CW00687286

Front cover, upper: Many photographs were taken of SMT buses leaving St Andrew Square bus station, Edinburgh. In light green, with =Scottish= fleetnames, BB52 heads for Hopetoun Cross Roads. *Iain MacGregor*

Front cover, lower: The Seddon Pennine VII with Alexander Y type bodywork was closely associated with Eastern Scottish in its later years. S834, a 1978 delivery with long-windowed body, heads through East Saltoun on its way to Gifford when new. *Harry L Barker*

Back cover, upper: Between 1956 and 1966, the Bristol Lodekka was SMT's standard double-decker. AA852 starts out from Edinburgh on the long journey to Glasgow via Bellshill in May 1970. This is a late model LD6G, new in 1961; this type was chosen by Scottish Bus Group after the FS model had been introduced. *Harry Hay*

Back cover, lower: The SMT name lived on after FirstGroup was formed and no.1209, a 1993 Volvo B10B with Alexander Strider 51-seat bodywork on service 16 to Blackridge at the Gyle roundabout to the west of Edinburgh in 1996. *John Burnett*

HARRY L BARKER

CONTENTS

Previous page: Among the more unusual buses that passed through the SMT fleet was this 1963 AEC/Park Royal Bridgemaster, which came to the company new following the acquisition of Baxter's of Airdrie. BB962A is seen leaving Buchanan Street bus station in Glasgow. It lasted in the fleet for 10 years before it was transferred to Highland Omnibuses. *Harry Hay*

Above: SMT built five single-deckers for its own fleet in 1954 using parts from former London Transport utility Guy Arab double-deckers. A further 18 similar buses were built for Highland Omnibuses. The SMT examples spent much of their time in the Borders, returning to Edinburgh at the end of their lives. D2A is seen in 1962 in St Andrew Square, Edinburgh, off to Loanhead. *Photobus.*

First published 2004
ISBN 0-946265-36-4

Typeset in Times and Helvetica
Electronic page makeup by Jeremy Scott

Published by:
Bus Enthusiast Publishing Company
5 Hallcroft Close, Ratho, Newbridge
Midlothian EH28 8SD
Tel/Fax: 0131 333 2796
Email: enquiries@busenthusiast.com
Bus Enthusiast is an imprint of Arthur Southern Ltd.

INTRODUCTION

WRITING A BOOK on SMT, Scottish Omnibuses Ltd (SOL) or Eastern Scottish - call it what you will - is not an easy matter as the company went through so many different phases in its colourful history. What is not in doubt, however, is that the company proved to be one of the most important, certainly in Scotland, and also in a UK context in many respects. I have set out to illustrate the vehicles which graced this varied fleet, principally from the years after the war to 1985, when as a prelude to impending privatisation the part of the company was hived off to form Lowland Scottish, with various other depots and operations also passing to the then Midland, Central and Kelvin companies.

A quick trawl through the numerous vehicles operated, some with intricate detail differences, produced a table with a minimum of 314 different types and variations of bus operated during the 1946-85 period! Quite simply, even if photographs of them all had been available, a book of that size would not have been practically possible. I have therefore included vehicles which were new in the pre-1946 years, but operated postwar, as well as those bought in the post-1985 years to the end of the company as we knew it in 1999 as separate sections in their own right, not as detailed as the main period under consideration (but enough to create a flavour of the time).

Those central 40 years proved to be the heyday of the company, reflecting all that was good (and bad!). This is the story of the company as it was, with comments in places on some of the operational problems which undoubtedly existed and which indeed created types of bus that would otherwise not have taken to the streets, having been acquired at short notice or involved in body swaps due to late delivery of the originally ordered vehicles. SMT and its successor SOL suffered from a perennial shortage of buses particularly during the peak summer season, but also between Easter (when coaches were only licensed for two weeks) and June, when all coaches were put on the road for the summer. It is neither meant to be a history, nor an exhaustive fleetlist - these are covered elsewhere, and readers are referred to the book 'From SMT to Eastern Scottish' by D L G Hunter published by John Donald Publishers Ltd (ISBN 0 85976 159 2), and also for detailed vehicle information to the excellent PSV Circle fleet history PM7 covering the years 1936-78. Rather I want to capture the day-to-day spirit of the buses that served Edinburgh and the Lothians, the Borders and parts of the central belt of Scotland.

I reckon I have travelled on these buses probably making in excess of 8,500 different journeys from the 1950s to the present day, but mostly between the 1950s and the late 1970s. If that were not enough, there were 29 buses a day which either passed or terminated outside my parents' cottage in Pencaitland, East Lothian, every arrival keeping me alert just in case something unusual turned up - and not just from the SMT fleet! The shortage of buses meant that Ribble coaches on the joint Scotland to Lancashire services appeared rather than being sent to New Street on layover, plus buses from Western SMT (hijacked before they could return to Dumfries), Highland (on arrival from Inverness), ditto MacBraynes and Alexander, including one memorable journey on an Albion Aberdonian. Edinburgh Corporation and Stark's buses were commonplace, and the day following Baxter's acquisition in December 1962, its Regent V/Massey PVD 567 appeared resplendent in blue.

If that special experience of travelling on or seeing an SMT bus is even remotely transferred to the reader I will have succeeded in my task!

Even with a detailed knowledge of the fleet I just never knew what the next bus to arrive would be, such was the variety and the unpredictable nature of its operations, most notably in the Edinburgh area.

The various headings are arranged in vehicle manufacturer order, roughly covering the timespan during which they became important or relevant. Hopefully this brings out the semblance of a vehicle policy, but perhaps it does camouflage the fact that between 1964 and 1971 the AEC Reliance 470, Albion Viking, AEC Reliance 590, Bristol RE, Bedford VAM5 and VAM70, Bristol LH6P, Leyland Leopard and Bedford YRQ were all purchased in succession, defying anybody to spot a single-deck vehicle policy. It was, however, there. Brief tables describe the vehicles themselves and cover all those buses purchased new, together with those purchased secondhand deliberately to be part of the fleet. Those acquired, for example, with the Baxter's or Lowland businesses, or which came into the fleet due to vehicle swaps, or those regarded as one-offs and which perhaps came into the fleet by accident, may not always be detailed although fleetlists of Lowland Motorways, Baxter's and Stark's are detailed as at the takeover dates. At the same time, I have attempted to illustrate a sufficiently wide selection of these vehicles to allow an accurate representation of these buses to flow to you.

The end of SMT. As this book went to press, the original SMT/Eastern Scottish operator's licence was surrendered to the Traffic Commissioner.

PM0000007 SI **License not continued WEF 03 May 2004**
(1768) **EASTERN SCOTTISH OMNIBUSES LTD T/A FIRST EDINBURGH**
DIRECTOR(s): H SCOTT, D MULHOLLAND, M J MITCHELL, A R GALL.

WESTFIELD AVENUE EDINBURGH EH112QH
Registered Bus Services running under this licence have also been set to CNS with immediate effect.

SMT – THE EARLY DAYS

The Scottish Motor Traction Co. Ltd. (SMT) was incorporated on 13 June 1905 with the specific purpose of operating motorbuses from the centre of Edinburgh to the Lothians, and in these days that included present-day city suburbs such as Corstorphine, to where the first bus ran on New Year's Day 1906. The company's routes quickly expanded to include Queensferry, Barnton and Cramond to the west, and within a year services to Dalkeith and Penicuik had been introduced, but journeys to the east of Edinburgh were somewhat later to appear (in 1912) although a tours programme to East Lothian had been started some years earlier. Tours, initially worked by charabancs, became an extremely important part of the overall operational picture with Edinburgh becoming a major international tourist centre, the company's coaching activities only declining in importance during the 1980s.

While growth was organic at the outset and the company was profitable in order to finance this, the rapid expansion and acceptance of local travel by means other than horseback or horse-drawn vehicle meant that numerous other bus companies sprang up in the surrounding towns. One of the first acquisitions was rather further afield, in the Angus area when Burke's Dundee & District Mechanical Transport service was purchased in 1920. These operations expanded under SMT, but were logically handed over to Alexander's shortly after nationalisation in 1949. The appetite for buying-out local operators had now been whetted, and there were numerous takeovers initiated (many involving some very small operators with only a handful of buses) which were a feature of the company's make-up right through until 1964, when Stark's of Dunbar succumbed. Such was the clamour to expand that SMT could in many ways be likened to present-day Stagecoach, rapidly becoming a dominant operator, enforcing its livery (until the Baxter's episode in 1962) on to the unsuspecting locals. Perhaps the most famous acquisitions were that of Coast Line in January 1937, a BET company based in Musselburgh, and whose buses survived up to 1960 in rebodied form; Lowland Motorways of Glasgow in January 1958; Baxter's of Airdrie in December 1962; and the aforementioned Stark's in January 1964.

In 1929, prior to the 1930 Road Traffic Act, SMT acquired a controlling interest in two growing companies, Alexander of Falkirk and Midland of Airdrie, thereby giving it a heavy presence in the central belt of Scotland. As will be revealed, the decision to control the Airdrie services from Edinburgh, rather than say pass them to Central SMT in Motherwell, was probably a mistake, as the cultures of the east and west of Scotland are very different from each other. Both the LMS and LNER railways took between them 50% control, also in 1929, and a year or two afterwards this resulted in some uneconomic train services being withdrawn, like those from Edinburgh to Lanark and Gifford, with SMT bus replacements being provided. Fleet strength rose to around 750 immediately after World War 2, further increasing to well over 900 in the peak years of the early 1950s as services were increased in frequency and coaching activities rose after the war, falling back slightly after Suez, but always hovering around this figure due to the acquisitions at the time, and in the future.

An SMT Maudslay ML3 of the mid-1920s passes the company's office at 45 Princes Street, Edinburgh, in the late 1920s. Note the parcels barrow parked at the kerb. *Gavin Booth collection*

LIVERIES, FLEETNAMES & FLEETNUMBERS

FROM 1930 until prior to nationalisation the standard SMT livery was two shades of blue and cream, which usually looked smart. Coaches had a blue roof and side flash, the remainder being cream. After nationalisation in 1949, two shades of green (dark and mid) and cream were tried, possibly to distinguish SMT vehicles from the much bigger fleet of blue Alexander buses. The internal colour schemes also changed simultaneously - blue-delivered buses having red interiors, green buses now having green seats and interior lining panels, dual-purpose vehicles floral brown seats, and London coaches grey seats.

It is true to say that SMT never became comfortable with its green liveries and this initial scheme only lasted just over two years. In 1952 a light green and cream was applied, the green being similar to that of Southdown, but not quite so rich, and the cream not so creamy, but its application perhaps left something to be desired. The cream roofs and green window surrounds, with hindsight, would have looked better if reversed to green roofs and cream window surrounds, but that never happened until it was too late - some Baxter's vehicles being painted into this style for a short period in 1962/3. Coaches were generally cream with

A reminder of the pre-1949 blue SMT livery is provided by the preserved J66, a 1942 Leyland Titan TD5 with body by Alexander to Leyland design. It is seen at Silverknowes, Edinburgh, on a local running day. *Gavin Booth*

Wearing the light green/cream livery that many will remember, and with *=Scottish=* fleetnames, two of the handsome AEC Regent III bought in 1949/50. BB79, on the left, has a Duple body, and BB94 has a Burlingham body. *Iain MacGregor*

green window surrounds and waistband, although to suit their body styles early coaches such as the Burlingham Seagulls and some Alexander-bodied Regal IVs had large green side areas within their curvaceous mouldings.

In early summer 1956 a very short-lived revival of two shades of green (dark and light) and cream was introduced for around six months, and was applied to some recently-delivered Bristol Lodekkas and some AEC Regals, the latter having a dark green side flash. By 1957, however, a determined return to the light green was made in a similar style to 1952-6, although halfcab single-deckers had their side flash painted cream rather than plain light green. Dark green (known as Humber Green), however, was retained for mudguards on front-engined vehicles, both single- and double-deck.

The light green was, apparently, not a good-wearing paint (or so the story goes) and rarely looked shiny for more than a few weeks, which was certainly true, and so in 1963/4 some further livery experiments appeared encompassing a variety of styles, and yet again some very short-lived two shades of green (dark and light) and cream vehicles emerged (dark green roof, cream windows and waistband, rest light green) notably on some 1959 Lodekkas and Park Royal Reliances from the B690-709 batch which were passing through Marine Works at the time for their five-year repaint. These only lasted a few weeks, but were extremely attractive. In late 1963 vehicles from the B917-22 batch, AEC Reliances with modern Alexander Y type bodies, came out in various liveries with a new hard-wearing dark green paint called Lothian Green, darker and very much richer than Tilling Green, although B919 did have Tilling Green applied experimentally. Likewise Park Royal-bodied AEC Monocoach B507 emerged in Lothian green bus livery (unusually with =Scottish= fleetname, this livery usually being seen with the later Eastern Scottish name, apart from on 1964 Reliances B78-92) and ran around for some time while the company made up its mind. In 1964 it was decided that Lothian Green was the colour to go for, and it would be applied in three styles: bus livery, where the whole vehicle apart from a cream waistband was green; dual-purpose livery (never applied to date, single-deckers being regarded as either buses or coaches) where the whole bus was green apart from a deep cream band below the central waistband, but with a green skirt (this style of livery, but using Tilling Green, was subsequently adopted by Bristol Omnibus for its one-man single-deckers, and Maidstone & District also copied it!); and coach livery, all cream apart from Lothian Green waistband and windows. So the company had again avoided cream window surrounds! It was only in the early 1980s that cream window surrounds appeared in an effort to brighten up the livery. After 1985 a reintroduction of two shades of green, with substantially more cream was introduced, the light green taking the form of a waistband on both double and single-deckers, but it did not look quite right, and became shabby fairly quickly.

However, as I write there is a remnant of the blue livery, which the company appeared reluctant to let go. Even in FirstBus days, it still exists. The company is famous for its paper destination stickers, most commonly used in the Edinburgh area on coaches without proper destination screens, but often used on stage service and on vehicles running from New Street depot which were not allocated there - therefore effectively covering just about every bus in the fleet at some time or other. The printing on these is blue, and can be traced back to prewar days when the blue livery existed. Around 1957, possibly as part of the determined effort to finally opt for light green, a whole tranche of stickers was printed with destinations in light green, but they had insufficient visibility for intending passengers and further orders were blue and these remain to this day. Many green stickers lasted for years, especially those with only rarely-used destinations such as Traprain, Glenkinchie and Yester.

The company also appeared to have difficulty with its fleetname. The SMT diamond had appeared in its earliest forms on tours publicity and route maps virtually from the start, but the non-diamond legend 'S.M.T.' was initially clearly emblazoned on the sides of buses. From 1935 certain coaches had the famous SMT diamond applied, but 'S.M.T.' still appeared without a diamond, sometimes in various sizes, on buses right through the war and up to 1950 on buses, the final vehicles delivered without diamond fleetnames being the Burlingham-bodied AEC Regent IIIs which were unique in having this feature with the green (dark and mid) livery. The diamond soon became universal, and was the hallmark of the company, but the non-diamond fleetname lingered on until 1954 in some remoter parts of the operating territory. Coaches in the early 1950s had the diamond applied with aluminium ribbing.

Prior to nationalisation SMT also operated the SMT Sales & Service car and truck/bus dealership and an agreement had been struck allowing the buses to continue to use SMT as a fleetname for a period thereafter, but the legal name of the company became Scottish Omnibuses Ltd (SOL). It had to happen - in 1959 a scripted version of Scottish Omnibuses appeared on vehicles in coach livery in the waistband 'flash' along with the SMT diamond on the vehicle sides, as a prelude to dropping SMT altogether. All coaches delivered in 1961 and 1962 had 'Scottish Omnibuses' fleetnames with no SMT at all. In 1963, in preparation for abandoning the SMT name as part of the agreement with the dealer side of the business (which remained in private hands) the word =Scottish= with wings either side appeared and was quickly applied to virtually the whole fleet. Then it appeared to dawn on someone that

=Scottish= really meant nothing and inferred it covered the whole of Scotland and so after about a year the SMT diamond was resurrected. At this time the change in livery to Lothian Green was just under way and for a short period it was possible to see Lothian Green buses with SMT fleetnames; immediately prior to that approximately 20 wore Lothian Green and =Scottish= fleetnames. Then in late 1964 'Eastern Scottish' was devised, applied in traditional Tilling underlined format, early examples being in a golden brown colour which did not stand out on the dark green, and was later changed to cream.

In line with all Scottish Bus Group companies in an effort to promote a corporate image, three-quarters of the Scottish Saltire and the words 'Eastern Scottish' in blue was applied in a large style in 1978, following the very successful corporate blue and white London livery introduced in 1976. The blue and green did not go together and in my opinion it ruined the appearance of the buses, always having to be applied on cream, and this marked the initial decline of the company.

The fleet numbering scheme has three components - a prefix, a number and a depot code suffix. The prefix had at least one letter, and at times up to four! In reverse, the final prefix letter denoted the chassis manufacturer - eg A for Bristol, B for AEC, C for Bedford, D for Guy and later Daimler, E for Daimler in 1958-60, H for Leyland single-deckers (later L from 1984), J for Leyland double-deckers (prewar - but carried over to Highland in the 1950s), K for Albion (also A and S), N for Leyland National, S for Seddon and V for Volvo. Double-deckers had the code doubled - therefore AA was a Bristol double-decker. A few months after the introduction of the dual-purpose Lothian Green livery in late 1964 a scheme was devised to differentiate coaches from semi-coaches and buses, with the first letter being significant: thus X - toilet coach, Y - a non-toilet coach and Z - a dual-purpose vehicle. Therefore ZB was a dual-purpose AEC single-decker. When Citylink was developed as a brand and SOL vehicles were painted in Citylink livery, C appeared between the chassis letter and type letter so that XCMM was a toilet coach, in Citylink livery, being a double-deck MCW Metroliner. There then followed the number, which from 1957 generally matched the registration number.

There was always a temptation to revert back to the number 1 for special vehicles, particularly coaches, and this tended to create havoc as it was practised on a random basis in 1954, 1955, 1961, 1962, and 1965, with fleetnumbers naturally reverting to 11 (not 1) in 1964 after having reached 964 in 1963 (although they were later to go up to 999). The reason 11 was chosen was due to the numbering of the 'Sir Walter Scott' class of Burlingham-bodied Reliances in 1961 as B1-10, but the company 'forgot' about the one-off B11 (YSF 242) delivered in 1962, and therefore two number 11s were in the fleet from 1964 to 1973 (although some other numbers under 50 were duplicated). The suffix letter denoted the depot code, and a separate chapter deals with these. The fleetnumbers were very accurately applied. I have ignored the prefixes other than that relating to the chassis manufacturer as status between coach, semi-coach and bus varied throughout a vehicle's life.

In 1956 a brief return to two shades of green and cream was made as applied to AA6A, a 1956 Bristol LD6G with ECW H60R bodywork in St Andrew Square when new. Some of this batch was delivered in all light green, and at least one subsequently had dark green window surrounds added afterwards, identifiable by the painting out of the black ribbing. *Photobus*

A maroon/cream livery was chosen for the Scott-class AEC Reliances with Burlingham Seagull 70 bodies bought in 1961. They all carried names relating to Sir Walter Scott's novels. B2, Ivanhoe, is seen on Tyneside on an extended tour.

Newly delivered in1963, Bristol Lodekka FS6G, AA948 shines in the sun. It has an offside illuminated advertisement panel, as yet unused. *R L Wilson/OTA*

From 1964, the darker Lothian Green was used as the principal colour for Eastern Scottish buses, complete with the Tilling-style underlined fleetname. AA208G, one of the 25 longer FLF6G Lodekkas, approaches Dalkeith bus station on one of its familiar haunts, the Edinburgh-Birkenside service. *Gavin Booth*

Noted in the west is B16V, a 1956 Reliance MU3RV with Alexander B45F body, originally Baxter's but repainted into light green livery shortly after the 1962 takeover, and displaying the =Scottish= fleetname. Such repaints of Baxter buses differed from the main single-deck fleet in having cream window surrounds and green roofs, rather than the other way round, the company believing this would identify buses on Baxter routes from standard SOL vehicles. It didn't and Baxter buses soon went back into blue livery! *Iain MacGregor*

Following the management buy-out a Seddon bus displays the revised dark green and cream livery with modernised (and attractive) SMT diamond logo. Taken in spring 1995, this livery was to remain short lived, but was probably one of the most attractive. *John Burnett*

The final nationalised Eastern Scottish livery yet again (for the fourth time!) reverted to two shades of green, with much more cream, and Seddon Pennine VII S625A, one of the 1979 batch of 40 B53F vehicles, is in St Andrew Square. The central light green band wore very badly and vehicles soon took on an unkempt appearance. *Photobus*

The Grampian style of livery, using a cream background and shades of green, was adopted under GRT ownership. No.949, seen in Musselburgh, is a former Northampton Transport East Lancs-bodied Leyland Olympian, and came to SMT via the parent Grampian fleet, already wearing these colours, so only a change of fleetname was required. *Gavin Booth*

Perhaps the least attractive livery of all was applied shortly after the Grampian style went out of favour when FirstBus came on the scene. Without any sympathy to the design of the bus, a Seddon passes through Musselburgh in a mainly cream scheme with green middle strip and black window surrounds. *John Burnett*

THE FLEET BEFORE 1946

TO COVER the vehicles prior to 1946 is an enormous task, because it was only in the late 1920s/early 1930s that a recognisable vehicle policy was pursued, and coupled with the numerous take-overs of smaller local operators, a large number of buses were individuals or unique in their own right. However, in the 1930s substantial numbers of new single-deckers entered service, mainly AEC Regals, and also Leyland Lions, Tigers and lightweight Cheetahs, along with Bedfords, which created a new era where Albions, Lothians, Reos, and Maudslays were just some of the chassis types no longer favoured. The 'modern' bus had arrived. Dual- or triple-sourcing was not necessary for the double-deckers, there being far fewer of them at this time, and a goodly number of all-Leyland Titans of various TD marques were supplied. Many of the single-deckers had bodies by Alexander, Metro-Cammell or Burlingham, the association with the latter continuing up to 1962.

When World War 2 arrived, those vehicles still on order were delivered, and both Regals and Tigers with Alexander bodies entered service up to 1940. During the war, 18 Regals and 18 Tigers were rebuilt to double-deck standard with new Alexander L53R bodies to enhance capacity, the London coach services not being operated in wartime. In addition the first two AEC Regents came in 1942, along with 22 utility Guys (with Gardner 6LW engines) with various makes of double-deck body, and a solitary Leyland TD5 in 1942, this having been constructed from spares at a time when the TD7 was the currently available model. Sixty B32F SMT-bodied Bedford OWBs arrived in 1944, and perhaps the oddest of all were six Dennis Lancet IIs with Strachan 35-seat single-deck bodies in 1943/44. Although the availability of Bristol after the war did change things, a common thread of vehicle policy can be found from the early 1930s to the late 1980s, with AECs, Bedfords and Leylands all featuring at one time or another in quantity. The illustrations here are not meant to be exhaustive, but to whet the appetite for what has still to come!

H5 is a very early 1929 Leyland Tiger, one of a batch of 12 delivered with Cowieson C29F bodies, but rebodied in 1938 by Alexander in its handsome B34R style, so typical of Scottish fleets. Note the SMT non-diamond fleetname. This bus lasted until 1954, but the rear entrance style lingered on until 1964 on identically-bodied new 1938 Regal Is. *Photobus*

35 AEC Regal Is (B130-54) came in 1935 with Alexander B32F bodies, and all but two were rebodied, 31 in Phase 1 and two in Phase 2 (see AEC single-deck chapter), leaving only two with original bodies, B130 and B151. The latter is noted in Princes Street post-1956 (note the dark green flash). It survived until 1958 and then went on to become a showman's bus. An Edinburgh 1954 PD2/20 with MCW Orion bodywork is in hot pursuit. *R H G Simpson*

Bedfords have always formed a large proportion of the touring fleet and a full extended tours programme was operated. C81A is a 1937 Bedford WTB with Duple C20F coachwork used on such tours, being one of 30 such vehicles. It was withdrawn in 1954.
Gavin Booth collection

Thirty-six vehicles were rebuilt as double-deckers between 1942 and 1945 to increase capacity (many previously having been used on the now-suspended London services), all with basic Alexander L53R bodies. Eighteen were Tigers, brought up to Titan TD5 standard, and the others were Regals rebuilt as Regents. In 1934 FS 8553 entered service as a 32-seat Burlingham bodied Regal coach, it survived in the form shown until 1957. *A B Cross*

AEC Regal I B193A was one of 15 similar vehicles delivered in 1938 with handsome Alexander B34R bodies, some unrebodied examples lasting until 1964, although this bus came off in 1961. With vehicles always being short in supply their suitability to the duties upon which they were used left something to be desired and around 1960, this veteran had just arrived in Edinburgh on the express service from Glasgow!
Gavin Booth

The standard new prewar double-decker was the all-Leyland TD5 with L53R bodywork, and HH45A charges along Princes Street in Edinburgh in two-tone green livery shortly before withdrawal in 1956 but looking in good condition. It was one of 20 delivered in 1938. An Edinburgh Metro-Cammell bodied Daimler CVG6 is in the background. *R H G Simpson*

Centre: In 1939 no fewer than 54 single-deckers were delivered of which 34 were Tiger TS8s, all with Alexander B34R rear entrance bodies, the last delivered to the company. (The others were AEC Regal Is with forward entrance bodies.) With a United Bristol L5G behind, H216E with non-diamond fleetname as late as March 1951, sits in Kelso Square having arrived from Berwick. Withdrawn in 1955, some of this batch went to Alexanders with the Dundee area services in 1949. *A B Cross*

Below: Among the utility vehicles to enter service during the war were 22 Guy Arab IIs, unusually with Gardner 6LW engines, and bodies by Roe, Massey, Brush, Northern Counties and Weymann. E18A awaits its next duty to Pathhead in St Andrew Square, in two-tone green, and was one of eight Weymann L55R examples delivered in 1945. *Photobus*

AEC SINGLE-DECKERS

FOR 20 YEARS after the war, there is no doubt the AEC single-decker epitomised the SMT/SOL fleet, and many hundreds entered service. Rather than simply plough through them all in one list, it is relevant to divide them up into appropriate sections to follow through the postwar vehicle policies pursued.

After the war SMT decided to standardise on AEC for most of its new single-deck service vehicles, thereby differing from its prewar policy of triple-sourcing Leyland, Bedford (for coaches) and AEC products, although Bedfords were still chosen for some coaches The post-war Regals modernised a large proportion of the fleet, and generally gave excellent service, the majority lasting up to 18 years in service often on front-line duty. The fact that fleetnumbers had reached B235 in 1946 indicates that 234 prewar AECs, mostly Regals (with a few acquired Rangers and original Reliances) had entered service in the 1930s, along with a slightly smaller number of Leyland Tigers and Bedfords. All of the Regals had the AEC 7.7-litre engine and crash gearbox, notwithstanding that double-deckers had pre-selective transmission and 9.6-litre engines.

AEC REGAL I AND III WITH ORIGINAL BODIES

AEC REGAL I 0662
7.7 litre engine, crash gearbox

FLEET	REGN NOS	YEAR	BODY
B235-59	ESC 429-53	1946 (25)	Duple B35F
B260-84	ESC 454-78	1947 (25)	Duple B35F
B285-309	FFS 182-206	1947 (25)	Alexander B35F

AEC REGAL III 0682 (6821A from B357 on)
7.7 litre engine, crash gearbox

FLEET	REGN NOS	YEAR	BODY
B310-44	FFS 207-41	1948 (35)	Alexander B35F
apart from B312/4/7/23/5/6/9/32/4/43 which were delivered as C30F for London service, upseated to B35F 1951/2			
B345-63	GSC 233-51	1948 (19)	Burlingham B35F
B364	GSC 457	1949 (1)	Burlingham FC31F (8ft wide)
B365-84	GSF 684-703	1949 (20)	Burlingham C35F
B385-99	GSF 704-718	1949 (15)	Alexander C30F for London service
B400-4	GSF 719-23	1949 (5)	Alexander B35F

Fifty-six AEC/Park Royal Monocoaches came in 1954/5, the first 31 being B45F. B433K is a late 1954 example looking very smart in Lothian Green working in the Borders near Peebles. SOL operated the largest fleet of Monocoaches anywhere, taking 95 new until 1957, and two secondhand from Alexanders. *John Burnett*

Seen in Newcastle is B276A, one of the second batch of 25 Duple B35F-bodied Regal Is delivered in 1947. Twenty-five identical vehicles had come in 1946. The bus is on the lengthy service from Newcastle to Edinburgh via Kelso. All the Duple-bodied Regals were rebuilt in 1953/4 as a result of the use of unseasoned timber. *R F Mack*

Fifty Duple B35F-bodied Regal Is were delivered in two equal batches in 1946/7. Here, B280A from the second batch arrives in central Edinburgh from Haddington. The shot can be dated to 1959 as the bus had just gone through its 12 year Certificate of Fitness (CoF) examination; an Alexander-bodied Guy Arab IV of Edinburgh is visible heading off down Leith Walk. *R H G Simpson*

In 1947 a further 25 Regal Is, but with Alexander B35F bodies, were delivered, represented by B290A travelling in from Lanark with a typical Lanark load! None of this batch was rebodied, the majority lasting well into 1964/5 giving good reliable service. Some retained their red seats (standard with the original blue livery) duly reupholstered until withdrawal. *R H G Simpson*

In 1948, 35 AEC Regal IIIs came with Alexander bodies, of which ten were C30F London coaches, and the rest were 35-seaters. An example of the latter is B335A, in two-tone green. The whole batch was rebodied in 1953, 20 with Burlingham Seagull bodies, and the remainder including this one with Dickinson FC35F bodies. *E Shirras*

Burlingham was also a favoured bodybuilder and 19 of these splendid Regal IIIs came in 1948 with B35F bodies, featuring side-facing seats over the rear wheelarches. B348F heads off to Bo'ness in West Lothian. *Photobus*

The first 8ft wide vehicle in the fleet was the unique B364, a 1948 Regal III with the forerunner of Burlingham's Seagull body built for the London service to FC31F layout. It had been standard practice for coaches to have 2+2 seating at the rear with a large armrest in the middle, but the additional 6in persuaded someone to fit five rear seats. Most subsequent non-toilet coaches, until 1970, however continued with the 2+2 pattern! It is seen here with its modified front grille. *Photobus*

Following the Park Royal-bodied AEC Monocoaches, SOL turned to Alexander and in 1956/7 received 39 examples with this style of body. B524 is seen on private hire duties in 1969. Note the alternate opening windows, ten of this batch being so fitted as an experiment to reduce draughts. The result was that all double-deckers from 1957 onwards had alternate sliders, but single-deckers did not receive this until 1960. *Harry Hay*

B775, an AEC Reliance 2MU3RV appeared at the Scottish Show in 1959 and was originally intended to be Alexander AC153. It retained some Alexander features including double width waistband incorporating rear registration number, false bumpers back and front (removed) and internally differing grab rails. It is seen in 1967 working to Selkirk. *John Burnett*

The 56 AEC Reliances with AV590 engines and Alexander Y type bodies were not the most popular vehicles with Eastern Scottish. Within seven years, half were cascaded to SBG's Highland and Northern companies. ZB113F is seen in Helensburgh; it had a short life too, but its withdrawal in 1970 followed a serious accident. *Harry Hay*

In 1949 came 20 Regal IIIs with halfcab Burlingham C35F bodies, which were extremely comfortable machines. They were well spread throughout the operating area. B372F is noted in St Andrew Square bus station. Sister vehicle B374 was rebodied in 1955 with the very last of the Alexander 1949 bodies displaced by Seagull rebodying as described in the text under Phase 2. *John Burnett*

The final halfcabs purchased new came in 1949 and were 20 Alexander-bodied Regal IIIs. The first 15 were to C30F layout for the London services, the final five being B35F in identical body shells. B393 is seen on service work in the Borders. The London coaches were all rebodied in 1954 with Burlingham Seagull bodies, but the five buses remained untouched until withdrawal in 1965/6, having been moved to the Borders. *R H G Simpson*

Alexander, Burlingham and Croft rebodied numerous prewar Regal Is between 1946 and 1948 under Phase 1, and here B164G represents the Alexander contingent. The chassis dates from 1935, the body from 1947. Later rebodied Alexander buses featured the more updated style with rounded window pans. As always the bus in the background is of interest, being one of Edinburgh's Leyland PD3s in the 261-4 batch, doubtless on the 19 circle. *Photobus*

AEC REGAL I AND III (REBODIED VEHICLES)

THERE WERE TWO distinct phases of rebodying the AEC Regal fleet after the war. In 1945 the company was faced with an enormous task of updating the fleet, and replacing the less sturdy and non-standard vehicles with new buses. However, what would otherwise have been time-expired buses had underneath them a chassis that after updating with lowered radiators etc would last for many years yet, and accordingly a number of better examples of both Regals and Tigers were chosen to be rebodied between 1946 and 1949. Both Alexander and Burlingham were mainly involved, and there were a few Croft bodies too, and these rebodied vehicles became almost indistinguishable from their new counterparts. They lasted for a further 10/12 years in service, and also enabled fleet replacement to be undertaken on a more even basis.

The second phase related to the advent of the underfloor-engined single-decker to the fleet in 1951, these rendering the halfcab fleet obsolete almost overnight. Because of the substantial and increasing tours programme, the desire to present a modern image resulted in a second rebodying exercise, more daring than the first, between 1952 and 1954. 15 Regal Is were involved in 1952, but otherwise all the others were Regal IIIs. All were lengthened to 30ft, and received 8ft-wide bodies, and all were given full fronts to try to simulate the look of contemporary underfloor-engined vehicles! Most were treated to the highly attractive Burlingham Seagull design, and SMT built up one of the largest Seagull fleets in the country as these fine bodies also went on to a number of Bedfords. Others were rebodied by Dickinson of Dunbar (possibly a device to get round the fact that these were new rather than simply rebuilt bodies) to a full fronted dual-purpose design. The bodies displaced from the Regal IIIs were cascaded on to other vehicles, but sadly it appears that a fully-detailed listing of what went where is not available. Some certainly went to Highland and Alexanders, and others appeared on rebodied Coast Line Tigers and SMT Regals not subject to the phase 1 exercise. Spares were held on jigs, the final one being used in 1955 on rebodying B374 after a crash. A handful of Regals and Tigers were rebuilt by ECW at its Irthlingborough works, the use of ECW to rebuild other vehicles in the fleet being repeated in 1969!

Burlingham 35-seat bus bodies were fitted to some Regal Is, and in two-tone green is B64J in the Borders on what would appear to be a workers' journey. The chassis was new in 1932, and it was rebodied in 1948.
Photobus

An example of the Croft-rebodied Regal Is B62WA of the same original batch as the vehicle above. These were allocated to Musselburgh depot and ran on the ex-Coastline route to Port Seton, their deep windows making the journey all the more pleasant. Note the stance 5 board in the background, and the WA depot code, abandoned in 1955.
Stewart J Brown collection

No fewer than 50 Regal Is and IIIs were lengthened to 30ft and rebodied between 1952 and 1954 with highly attractive Burlingham Seagull bodies. The first 15 were Regal Is with FC37F bodies, but in 1953 20 Regal IIIs with FC35F bodies appeared. B313A is in Edinburgh's Princes Street. Note the raised aluminium SMT fleetname. A further 15 came in 1954.
R H G Simpson

PHASE 1 REBODYINGS, 1946-9

B14-73 (FS 2251-310)
AEC Regal I/Alexander B34R, new 1932
Rebodied Alexander B35F 1946/8
B15/7, 23/5/9, 31/2/4-6/8/40/3/7/52/7/9-61/7/8,70 (22)
Rebodied Burlingham B35F 1948
B14/6/8-22/4/7/8/33/9/41/2/4-6/8-51/3/5/6/64-6/9,71/2 (30)
Rebodied Croft B35F 1948
B30/54/8/62/3/73 (6)

B93-122 (FS 8553-82)
AEC Regal I/Burlingham B34R, new 1934
Rebodied Alexander B35F 1948/9
B93,104/8-10/3/7 (7)

B130-54 (WS 4478-502)
AEC Regal I/Alexander B32F, new 1935
Rebodied Alexander B35F 1946-8
All except B130/41/51/3 (21)

B155-68 (WS 4503-16)
AEC Regal I/Cowieson B34R, new 1935
Rebodied Alexander B35F 1946-8
All (14)

B169 (WS 4517)
AEC Regal I/Alexander B38F, new 1936
Rebodied Alexander B35F 1948

The remaining 15 of the 1948 Regal IIIs were rebodied by Dickinson of Dunbar, who specialised in such work, but it is believed that much of the material was supplied from SOL's Marine Gardens. They too were 30ft long, and were intended for longer-distance stage services with only 35 plusher seats and various coach details such as the sliding door, poor destination equipment etc, and were the forerunner of the dual-purpose concept. B338A is at Whitesands, Dumfries - note the paper destination stickers (in blue!). *R H G Simpson*

PHASE 2 REBODYINGS, 1952-54
(Original details as above)

Burlingham Seagull FC37F 1952
B141/53/79/80/2-5/7/8/99, 207/9/26/30 (15)

Burlingham Seagull FC35F	1953	B310-29 (20)
SMT/Dickinson FDP35F	1953	B330-44 (15)
Burlingham Seagull FC35F	1954	B385-99 (15)

A number of other cascaded rebodyings from the original Regal IIIs are not recorded here. B228 was rebuilt by ECW.

A handful of bodies were only rebuilt, rather than treated to a full rebodying, and these went to ECW at Irthlingborough. B228A is a 1940 Regal I originally with Alexander B39F body, and while its frontal appearance is clearly of Alexander origin, the side windows give the ECW game away. The bus is heading for York Place, Edinburgh, bound for the East Lothian village of Ormiston, served today by lowfloor Dennis Dart SLFs. *Gavin Booth collection*

AEC UNDERFLOOR-ENGINED SINGLE-DECKERS

For bus and semi-coach work SMT effectively standardised on AEC single-deckers after the war right through until 1966, with the notable exception of 1965 when none was purchased. The full gallery of Regal IVs, Monocoaches (where the company was the largest operator in the country) and Reliance 470s and 590s are included. Some dual-sourcing was practised, especially relative to coaches when both Bedford and Bristols were purchased, the latter being the preferred make for heavy coaching work, and latterly Albion Viking. However the Reliances and Monocoaches formed the backbone of the single-deck bus fleet. Reliance 2MU3RA demonstrator WJU 407, with Willowbrook body, appeared in late 1960 to allow examination of its air brakes, and although the 1961 buses retained vacuum brakes (they had already been ordered), future vehicles had air brakes. The underfloor-engined AECs formed the largest sector in the postwar fleet. At least B671, 715 and 91 are preserved. There were numerous secondhand AECs that entered the fleet - these are by and large covered in the Lowland Motorways, Baxter's and Stark's chapters, with other one-offs in the chapter of that name. The tables reflect the position of the buses when delivered new.

FLEET	REGN NOS	YEAR	BODY
AEC REGAL IV 9821E (9822E*) 9.6-litre engine, 4-speed preselective gearbox			
B405-24/ 39-44	HWS 907-26/41-6	1951 (26)	Alexander C30Ft
B445-54	JSF 145-54	1952 (10)	Alexander C40F
B455-62	KSC 532-9*	1953 (8)	Alexander C30Ft
B463-79	KSC 540-56*	1953 (17)	Alexander C38F
AEC MONOCOACH MC3RV AH410 engine, 5-speed synchromesh gearbox			
B425-30	LSC 566-71	1954 (6)	Park Royal B45F
B431-8	LWS 875-82	1954/5 (8)	Park Royal B45F
B480-96	LWS 883-7/9-900	1955 (17)	Park Royal B45F
B497-521	LWS 901-25	1955 (25)	Park Royal DP41F
B522-46	NSG 813-37	1956 (25)	Alexander DP41F
B568-81	OWS	1957 (14)	Alexander DP41F
AEC RELIANCE MU3RV AH410 engine, 5-speed synchromesh gearbox			
B547	NSF 543	1955 (1)	Alexander C30Ft
AEC RELIANCE 2MU3RV AH470 engine, 5-speed synchromesh gearbox			
B658-69	RSC	1958 (12)	Park Royal DP41F
B670-89	SWS	1959 (20)	Alexander C38F
B690-709	SWS	1959 (20)	Park Royal DP41F
B710-8	SWS	1959 (9)	Park Royal DP41F
B775	USC	1959 (1)	Alexander DP41F
B776-809	USC	1960 (34)	Alexander DP41F
B810-34	WSC	1961 (25)	Alexander DP41F
B1-10	WSF 201-10	1961 (10)	Burlingham Seagull 70 C34F
B11	YSF 242	1962 (1)	Burlingham Seagull 70 C34F
B964	121 CVD	1962 (1)	Alexander DP41F
AEC RELIANCE 4MU3RA AH470 engine, 5-speed synchromesh gearbox			
B910	YWS	1961 (1)	Alexander Y C38Ft
B911-6	8911-6 SF	1963 (6)	Alexander Y C38Ft
B917-22	8917-22 SF	1963 (6)	Alexander Y DP49F
B50-60	AFS-B	1964 (11)	Alexander Y C40F
B61-5	AFS-B	1964 (5)	Alexander Y C45F
B66-77	AFS-B	1964 (12)	Alexander Y DP49F
B78-92	AFS-B	1964 (15)	Alexander Y B53F+24
AEC RELIANCE 2MU3RA AH470 engine, 5-speed synchromesh gearbox			
B895-909	YWS	1962 (15)	Alexander DP41F
B923-42	8923-42 SF	1963 (20)	Alexander Y DP41F
B93-99	AFS-B	1964 (7)	Alexander Y DP41F
B100-5	AFS-B	1964 (6)	Alexander Y C38F
AEC RELIANCE 2U3RA AH590 engine, 4-speed synchromesh gearbox			
B106-61	EWS-D	1966 (56)	Alexander Y DP49F

Twenty-six AEC Regal IV London toilet coaches came in 1951 with Alexander C30Ft (reclining seats) bodies replacing on a one-to-one basis the 26 Regal III London coaches delivered in 1948/9. They operated in this as-delivered two-tone green/cream livery for the first three seasons only going into allover cream with light green windows for the 1954 summer season. They featured Alexander's famous 'V' screens, first introduced on these fine coaches, and fitted by Alexander on all sorts of buses every year since until 1999. This is B411.
G H F Atkins

Over the years detail alterations to these coaches were made, but the 12-year CoF overhaul in winter 1962/spring 1963 saw the fitting of Dawson heaters and radiator alterations resulting in a well-proportioned grille being added to the front. The =Scottish= fleetname had not yet been introduced, but the following winter the SMT ribbed fleetname was removed and replaced. This therefore dates this picture of B406A in London to summer 1963.
R H G Simpson

Ten Regal IVs with similar Alexander bodies, but to C40F specification, came in 1952, also delivered in the two-tone livery, but repainted into cream coach livery within a matter of months. They were the first vehicles to feature the brown floral pattern seats, and remained in service until 1966. B451 leaves Edinburgh having been downgraded to bus duties in Lothian Green livery. Most of these vehicles had the opening driver's windscreen replaced in the early 1960s.
R H G Simpson

The 1953 Regal IV deliveries also contained a few London coaches but to a design only produced that year, and only for SOL. Towards the end of its life, B461A leaves on stage service to Oakbank, the use of such luxurious coaches on peak runs being commonplace due to the ever-present vehicle shortage. The fleetnumber is in the SMT diamond on the front, and the split windscreen remains intact. *R H G Simpson*

A similar body style, but with roof glasses and side mouldings, was fitted to 17 1953 Regal IV coaches with C38F bodies. Glass rain guards were introduced with the 1953 deliveries and remained until withdrawal on these vehicles. B465A is in Oxford. Some were withdrawn in 1963/4 and provided seats to upseat Bristol LS/MW coaches, but the rest went on until 1965/6 in dual-purpose livery applied without sympathy to the side mouldings. *R H G Simpson*

The first six AEC Monocoaches built, chassis numbers MC3RV001-6, came to SOL and B430A was the sixth. Their Park Royal B45F bodies were well-proportioned. The location is Platform E in St Andrew Square bus station, and the bus is about to take up the stance for Leven, a journey in excess of two hours. These had green moquette bus seats, standard on new buses until 1960. *Photobus*

The 25 Monocoaches delivered in 1956 had Alexander DP41F bodies. B534W is on Stand D13 and features opening windows on all nearside bays and most offside bays. Ten of this batch, however, experimented with alternate opening windows but such an arrangement was only practised on double-deckers from 1957, single-deckers keeping a full array of opening windows until 1960. Note the white background panel for the fleetname. *John Burnett*

The only AH410-engined AEC Reliance MU3RV purchased new by the Company was B547A, which despite its bus-outline bodyshell was fitted out to C30Ft standard for London service. Fuel saving was uppermost in the minds of management at the time, but it proved too noisy to be acceptable on night journeys. It was only sparingly used, and ended up as a driver trainer. *Photobus*

The first true dual-purpose vehicles in the fleet, and the first Scottish Bus Group buses to a DP41F layout (which later became a standard), were the final 25 1955 Park Royal Monocoaches. Initially used on longer-distance routes, these featured brown floral moquette seats to a Park Royal design. B519F is also in Platform E along with BB91A, a 1950 Burlingham-bodied Regent III and a 1956 Bristol LD6G, AA5A. *R H G Simpson*

The final AEC Monocoaches built were 20 1957 examples, of which the last six went to Highland. The first identical 14 came to SOL, and B579 is in Newcastle. All but three of this batch were prematurely withdrawn in 1969, not going through their second CoF, due to the need to overhaul some of the 1962 Bedford VAS1s as a result of late delivery of Bristol LH coaches that year. *R H G Simpson*

The company returned to Park Royal in 1958 for 12 DP41F Reliances, the Monocoach having been dropped by AEC. Although PSV Circle records these as MU3RV, they were in fact 2MU3RVs and had the AH470 engine. B664A is in Dumfries. Highland received earlier six similar vehicles, but MU3RVs. *Photobus*

A further 29 Park Royal-bodied Reliances came in 1959 of which the first 20 were in coach livery, but with DP41F bodies to a slightly more rounded design. In the first inkling of the abandonment of SMT as a fleetname, these also had 'Scottish Omnibuses' in the flash. B701A stands in the greasy squalor that was a trademark of St Andrew Square bus station after rain. The zebra crossing was generally ignored by drivers, and it was soon removed. *Photobus*

The final nine Park Royal Reliances were intended as buses, in this elaborate bus livery possibly inspired by British Railways DMU designs of the time. To the same body outline as B690-709 these did not have head-cushions. B717 was fitted with an AH410 engine at some time during its life. These never carried the 'Scottish Omnibuses' legend despite having plenty space in the flash to do so. *R H G Simpson*

Alexander bodied a further 20 Reliances in 1959 with unique C38F bodies. They had deeper windscreens, and the emergency exit was towards the rear of the bus rather than being in the middle, there being no seat pitch restrictions for the smaller capacity. These were always regarded as coaches, but were unusual in being AECs; Bristols had been favoured in the past and would be in the future. B673A is travelling from London to Edinburgh via the West Coast route. This particular bus was transferred to the Stark's fleet in 1964. *Gavin Booth*

The 1960 Reliances came in three lots - B775 (see page 16) was at the 1959 show, and B776-804 arrived in spring 1960. Their Alexander DP41F bodies were a huge improvement on their previous Park Royal stablemates. The final five were diverted from Highland, and Highland's five became B805-9 in early summer. They could be differentiated by the rearmost opening window being one bay forward on the Highland vehicles, as illustrated here on B782A and the bus next to it, the latter being an intended Highland vehicle! *R H G Simpson*

1961 saw 25 almost identical vehicles arrive, but intended as buses they appeared in bus livery without head-cushions, but this did not stop them venturing far and wide. B821B is in Union Street, Aberdeen, on a private hire. These did not carry 'Scottish Omnibuses' in the flash, being buses. *R H G Simpson*

Strategically posed beside the Forth Bridge in South Queensferry is B1A, the first of the 1961 Reliances with C34F Burlingham Seagull 70 bodies. All were in an attractive maroon and cream livery and were named after characters in the Sir Walter Scott novels. B1 was exhibited at the 1960 Commercial Motor Show, incorrectly registered WSS 201. An eleventh, B11A, came in 1962 from dealer stock to cover a football team contract (such was the tightness of the number of buses). The glass rooflights leaked, and were replaced fairly quickly. These vehicles were the first to totally avoid mention of SMT in the fleetname, and no other new coaches carried 'SMT' from now on. *Gavin Booth collection*

Only 15 Reliances were delivered in 1962, but they had fluorescent lighting and air-powered doors making them ideal for one-man working. B908J stops outside Kelso Abbey on a working to Cornhill prior to the introduction of 'Z' prefixes to denote a semi-coach placing this photo in late 1964/early 1965. Dual-purpose livery was only carried by a few vehicles with this body style in this batch. The bus, along with sisters B905-7 was transferred to Stark's in 1967, displaced at Berwick by Bedford VAM5s.
Gavin Booth

The purchase of the Baxter fleet on 1 December 1962 resulted in 121 CVD, a 1962 Reliance with the curved style of Alexander DP41F body, entering service for the first time with SOL from Edinburgh, never having been licensed by Baxter. It is seen in later life as ZB964A, having been fitted with route number blinds, which were not fitted when new. It was the last pre-Y type Alexander-bodied vehicle to enter service in the UK in 1963. *Photobus*

The prototype Y type was a unique London coach, B910, and was exhibited at the 1961 Scottish Motor Show. In apple green and gold, with a C38Ft layout, it did not have an above-windscreen destination screen, and the offside emergency door had a small out-of-place circular window, being in the toilet, this being quickly replaced. It was one of the very few 36ft long AH470-engined Reliances built with the 126hp engine, most others having the uprated 138 hp unit from 1963. It had a reputation for running out of fuel, and was downgraded to semi-coach status in 1969 (DP45F). It was used by Alexander for experimental purposes, and although worked by SOL, was not purchased until summer 1963 from Alexander.
Bus & Coach

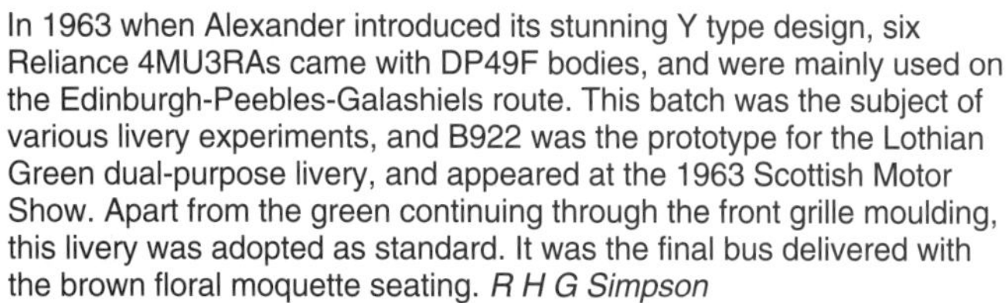

In 1963 when Alexander introduced its stunning Y type design, six Reliance 4MU3RAs came with DP49F bodies, and were mainly used on the Edinburgh-Peebles-Galashiels route. This batch was the subject of various livery experiments, and B922 was the prototype for the Lothian Green dual-purpose livery, and appeared at the 1963 Scottish Motor Show. Apart from the green continuing through the front grille moulding, this livery was adopted as standard. It was the final bus delivered with the brown floral moquette seating. *R H G Simpson*

Twenty short Y types with DP41F bodies, incorporating bus-style windows, also came in 1963. These improved passenger comfort dramatically being wider and longer than past buses. B932E leaves for Jedburgh in 1965, the route number being introduced in a total renumbering from 1 January 1965. Note the opening window arrangement, only bays two and four having sliders. This particular bus had an Eastern Scottish fleetname on the boot, the only known example of both a mixture, and Eastern Scottish on an unrepainted light green vehicle. *R H G Simpson*

Six different seating arrangements blessed the 56 1964 Reliances, all with Y type bodywork. The first 16 were coaches, B50-60 having only 40 luxurious grey 'London' coach seats with 2+2 rear seats, but B61-5 were C45F. Again only 'Scottish Omnibuses' was carried as a fleetname. B62A is in Princes Street. Note the half-depth door windows - a short-sighted SOL specification as these had to be altered to enable driver-only operation, drivers requiring a nearside view of the kerb. *R H G Simpson*

The next 12 were to DP49F specification, with red seats. B77A is seen in Fife having crossed the Forth Road Bridge on what was the very first stage carriage journey across in 1964. It is bound for Leven - not yet on the screens - with a Fife Bristol FS6G behind. B72F of this batch completed 1 million miles in service, apparently without breaking down. It was allocated to Linlithgow depot. *John Burnett*

Numerically the next 15 had B53F+24 bodies with short bus windows, but were the last delivered towards the year-end. They brought the number of 4MU3RA models up to 56, a number that keeps cropping up. Four each went to Bathgate, Linlithgow, and New Street respectively, with the final three going to Hawick. Reallocation proved to be fairly swift and here B89E is astride Kirk Yetholm green, the end of the Pennine Way, taking its 50-minute layover before connecting with the United Wooler-Yetholm Saturday-only service. *Harry L Barker*

The final six were short coaches, seating 38. They however had been intended for Highland and would have been that company's first Y types, but the acquisition of Stark's of Dunbar produced four Thames Trader coaches which, along with some Bedfords, went to Highland instead. Poor old Highland! B101A is seen in Princes Street when new. B103 was fitted with an experimental cooling system towards the end of its life - a bit late perhaps! *R H G Simpson*

Only seven short Reliances with DP41F bodies arrived in 1964. ZB95W is parked up on a hire in the late 1960s prior to being converted to driver-only and moved to Edinburgh. The positioning of the fleetname beggars belief, the flash remaining empty, but this was repainted into Lothian Green (from light green coach livery) prior to the introduction of cream fleetname transfers, so there was some reasoning behind the cream background positioning! *R H G Simpson*

No Reliances were purchased in 1965, the AH470 engine having fallen out of favour. However, the AH590 continued and 56 entered the fleet in 1966, in two main batches. ZB106 was at the 1965 Scottish Show and featured a sickly brown interior trim, and ZB107-31 arrived in the spring, with ZB132-61 following in autumn 1966. With 153hp, these were by far the fastest vehicles in the fleet and produced sound effects that have yet to be bettered. The front bumpers were quickly removed both by accident and, latterly, on purpose. Many went to Highland and Northern as cooling problems unfortunately persisted, and in 1973 SOL faced the difficulty of overhauling all the 1966 vehicles. These were the final AECs to enter the fleet. *R H G Simpson*

AEC DOUBLE-DECKERS

IMMEDIATELY AFTER the war AEC was also chosen as the standard for double-deckers, this marking a distinct departure from the prewar Leyland Titan choice. During the war 18 Regal I London coaches had been rebuilt as Regents and rebodied by Alexander to L53R layout, and two unfrozen Regents were delivered. The advent of the Regent III, very similar to London's RT, proved irresistible and no fewer than 80 entered service between December 1947 and 1950. As the coach fleet was renewed or rebodied, there followed a long gap until 1956 before any further double-deckers came into the fleet, but by that time the Bristol Lodekka was the natural choice, SMT requiring lowbridge, or lowheight vehicles. The only other AEC double-deckers to come new into the fleet were a Bridgemaster and Renown, whose stories are told in the captions, these being connected with the Baxter takeover. All of Baxter's other AEC deckers migrated to Edinburgh, including another Bridgemaster and two Regent Vs.

Right: In early 1948, a very welcome delivery of 40 AEC Regent IIIs with spartan but sturdy Alexander L53R bodies was made. BB21 was the first, registered ESC 421 but when that registration was spotted on a motorcycle, the bus was re-registered FWS 571. These buses had a very long life and were popular with drivers due to their preselective gearboxes. *R H G Simpson*

Below: A further 20 Regent IIIs but with Duple L53R 8ft-wide bodies arrived in 1949, the first double-deckers in the fleet to this width. They did not have a central cream band, but rather aluminium ribbing which made them look drab in Lothian Green. BB69 leaves St Andrew Square bus station on an Edinburgh-worked journey to Penicuik, the bus being allocated to Broxburn. The bus had either been released from the Marine Works and was being used by New Street, or Broxburn had responded to a request for weekend buses by sending in one of its oldest!

The 1950 delivery of 20 Regent IIIs had curvaceous Burlingham bodies, also to L53R layout. Apart from having an alarming tendency to keel into the side on even a modest camber, they were the first SBG buses to feature the hexagonal destination box. Because no further double-deckers entered the fleet until 1956, it was not adopted as an SBG standard until then. BB85A is parked in front of BB89 in Edinburgh.
R H G Simpson

Below, left: When Baxter's was taken over, two Bridgemasters were virtually complete at Park Royal intended to be Baxter's 79/80 (479/80 DVA). The new AEC Renown had just been announced at the 1962 Commercial Show, and because of known teething troubles with Albion Lowlanders entering SBG fleets, AEC was desperate to have Renowns in SBG service. They offered to try to sell the Bridgemasters and replace these with Renowns and even allocated chassis numbers 3B3RA024/5 to the vehicles. 479 DVA went to Red Rover, Aylesbury as 6116 BH, but the other could not be placed. It was therefore down-seated to 70 (from 72), reupholstered with standard red moquette, opening vents were fitted to the front upper deck windows, and it entered SOL service as BB962A (9962 SF) incredibly retaining Baxter's non-standard destination box, subsequently replaced with a hexagonal one some years later. The second Renown was built, as 3B3RA025 (chassis 024 was never built, the number being left vacant) and became BB963A (9963 SF). BB962A, with BB18A behind, heads south from Edinburgh on North Bridge, while the Renown accelerates out of the bus station to Balerno.
Gavin Booth collection/ John Burnett

FLEET NOS.	REGN. NOS	YEAR	BODY
AEC Regent III 0961 (9612E from BB55) 9.6-litre engine, preselective gearbox			
BB21	FWS 571	1947 (1)	Alexander L53R
BB22-60	ESC 422-8, FFS 150-81	1948 (39)	Alexander L53R
BB61-80	GSF 644-63	1949 (20)	Duple L53R
BB81-100	GSF 664-83	1950 (20)	Burlingham L53R
AEC Bridgemaster 2B3RA AH590 engine, 4-speed synchromesh gearbox			
BB962	9962 SF	1962 (1)	Park Royal H70F
AEC Renown 3B3RA AH590 engine, 4-speed synchromesh gearbox			
BB963	9963 SF	1963 (1)	Park Royal H74F

THE BEDFORDS

SMT ALWAYS APPEARED to have a soft spot for Bedfords. The first came into the fleet in 1930, and by the start of the war, 95 were in stock, the majority being used as coaches. During the war no fewer than 60 OWBs, with SMT B32F bodies to a design very similar to Duple were acquired, but they did not last long, most going by 1949, due to body rot resulting from the use of unseasoned timber. Following the war, the lighter coach duties were still trusted to Bedfords, and while Bristol latterly became the favoured coach chassis manufacturer in the 1950/60s, Bedfords returned to the fleet in a big way between 1967 and 1975 when numerous examples took to the roads, initially as an ideal one-man operated vehicle for the Borders, but latterly appearing on most types of duty in the fleet.

A number of the postwar OBs were rebodied by Burlingham with its Baby Seagull body, in a similar fashion to the AEC Regals noted earlier. The introduction of the innovative Border Courier services in 1978, where rural routes ran between hospitals and provided a service at the same time, resulted in some CFLs and VAS vehicles with parcels compartments joining the fleet. These services still run today.

FLEET	REG NOS	TYPE	YEAR	BODY
C156-68	FFS 856-68)	OB	1947 (13)	SMT C29F
C169-87	FFS 869-87)	OB	1947 (19)	SMT C25F
C188	JS 7799)	OB	1948 (1)	SMT C29F
Ex Mackenzie, Garve, 1949				
C156-75 (FFS 856-75) were rebodied in 1953 with Burlingham Baby Seagull C24F bodies				
C189-208	JSF 814-33	SB	1952 (20)	Burlingham Seagull C30F
C1-20	YWS 850-69	VAS1	1962 (20)	Duple Bella Vista C24F
C232-51	HSF-E	VAM5	1967 (20)	Alexander Y B45F
C252-71	LFS-F	VAM70	1968 (20)	Duple (Midland) DP41F
C450-60	USF-J	YRQ	1971 (11)	Alexander Y DP45F
C461-75	BFS-L	YRQ	1972 (15)	Alexander Y DP45F
C511-20	BSG-L	YRQ	1973 (10)	Alexander Y DP45F
C564-70	RFS-M	YRQ	1974 (7)	Alexander Y C38F
C571/4-8	SFS-N)	YRQ	1974 (6)	Alexander Y C38F
C572/3	SFS 403/4N	YRQ	1974 (2)	Alexander Y C38F
C717-21	LSG-P	YRQ	1975 (5)	Alexander Y C38F
C722-6	LSG-P	YRQ	1975 (5)	Alexander Y DP45F
C727-36	MSF-P	YRT	1975 (10)	Alexander Y DP49F
C737-46	MSF-P	YRT	1975 (10)	Alexander Y B53F
C1-5	HSU-T	CFL	1978 (5)	Reebur DP13F + parcels
C6-10 (FFS-X)		VAS5	1981 (5)	Reebur DP17F + parcels

The acquisition of MacKenzie of Garve provided an almost identical bus to SOL's own OB coaches in July 1949, new in 1948. It became C206, but due to the cancelled OBs it was, unusually for SOL, renumbered to C188 in 1952. It did not have an aluminium SMT diamond, and tended to be regarded as a freak, with a later reduced C24F capacity. It was mainly used as a staff bus between New Street depot and St Andrew Square but occasionally made a foray on peak service as seen here off to Oakbank. The bus following is a Coastline rebodied Tiger H209W. These were the days! *Photobus*

Following delivery of 60 Bedford OWBs during the war with utility SMT bus bodies, 32 OBs with SMT-built Duple Vista style coach bodies came in 1947, both 25- and 29-seaters. The last was C187, a C25F example seen in two-tone green with aluminium SMT diamond. These could be differentiated from true Duple bodies as the door slid inside the vehicle, rather than outside. The original order had been for 50 such vehicles, but the final 18 were cancelled. *R H G Simpson*

In 1953, 20 of the OBs were converted to forward control at New Street and rebodied by Burlingham with Baby Seagull FC24F bodies, and C174A shows the clean and attractive lines of these coaches which were mainly used on extended tours. They were replaced on a straight one-for-one basis in 1962 with 20 VAS/Duple coaches of the same capacity, which meant that tour seating plan sheets did not have to be altered! Now were the priorities correct? *Photobus*

Waverley Bridge in Edinburgh is the setting for this shot of C201A, one of 20 Bedford SBs with Burlingham Seagull C30F bodies, also used on extended tours. It is passing an Edinburgh all-Leyland Royal Tiger vehicle, converted to a coach from a rear entrance bus, and used for many years on the Edinburgh City Tour duties. *Photobus*

A gap of nine years passed before further Bedfords entered the fleet, and C2 turns off Princes Street showing off its classic Duple Bella Vista design. They replaced Seagull-bodied OBs as mentioned above, but were scheduled to retire without being overhauled in 1969. The late arrival of Bristol LHs delayed this for many of them by a year after receiving quick CoF patch-ups. C6 was repainted into the maroon and cream livery, also adorned by B1-11, for one season in 1968. These vehicles never carried an SMT fleetname. *R H G Simpson*

The search of many years for a truly rural bus ended in 1967 when 20 VAM5s with Alexander B45F bodies arrived. These spent the first four or five months working on urban and interurban routes from Edinburgh, without driver-only equipment, sound-deadening or Edinburgh destination screens. C242E is on the normally double-deck service 70. Note again the opening window arrangement, this time only bays two and six are fitted with hoppers. Bay four was, for reasons unknown, deliberately left fixed. After the Reliance 590s, these buses were a rude awakening for many. All went to Borders depots, where they remained. *Gavin Booth*

The 20 1968 Bedford VAM70s had Willowbrook (but with Duple Midland plates) DP41F bodies and a handful were allocated to Edinburgh to inter-work with Borders depot driver-only services. They provided a welcome change from the Y type. ZC257A is noted in June 1968 about to depart to Hopetoun House with a typical paper sticker and a blank destination screen. Again note the opening window sequence! *Gavin Booth*

The majority of the 1968 VAM70s went to the Borders. ZC266D, with Willowbrook DP41F body, stands in rainy Selkirk about to depart on the town service. *R L Wilson*

The 1974 YRQs were all delivered as C38F (with 2+2 rear seating) and continued the tradition of Bedford coaches in the fleet, having been a feature since the 1930s. All were subsequently converted to B45F layout, but here, when new and not equipped for driver-only operation. YC576A is noted in a posed manufacturer shot. *Vauxhall Motors Ltd*

The initial 1975 order was for 10 YRQs, five each of C38F coaches, and DP45F semi-coaches, but the latter came in coach livery for one season due to a shortage of coaches. YC718A, fitted with non-reflective registration plate, has arrived from South Queensferry as a driver-only bus working up Bus Grant mileage. The attractive brown and yellow checked coach seats can be seen. *John Burnett*

New Border Courier buses came in 1981 in the form of five Bedford PKJ (VAS5) with Reeve Burgess bodies, and ZC9 was photographed in typical borders terrain. *Gavin Booth Collection*

BRISTOL SINGLE-DECKERS

FOLLOWING NATIONALISATION IN 1949, the products of Bristol and ECW were openly available to Scottish Bus Group companies. However, the Scottish situation differed from that of the Tilling group in that other makes of vehicle could also be purchased and therefore (apart from the likes of Sheffield where the railway-controlled fleet could also specify Bristol/ECW vehicles, and in theory London Transport - in practice both undertakings took ECW bodies only) the Bristol/ECW marques were effectively available to SBG on the same basis as the products of, say, AEC and Leyland. This often resulted in the Scottish Bus Group receiving preferential attention when delivery dates were concerned, and there is little doubt that when matters got seriously behind at ECW in the 1963-66 period, the Scottish fleets fared very well indeed at the expense of the Tilling fleets. It also resulted in some detail differences to Scottish buses, some of which were incorporated into standard ECW designs, notably the inward-opening door on LS coaches, and below-windscreen destination screens. A622 was the very first Bristol MW coach built, entering service even prior to Crosville's prototype! With SMT it is of note that every Bristol single-decker delivered new to the company came as a coach, in line with its vehicle policy to use AEC mainly as a semi coach and bus provider (although there were AEC coaches), and Bristol and Bedford as coach suppliers, at least until the mid-1960s. Most of the Bristols were downgraded during their lives to work as semi-coaches. For ease of reference, I have incorporated the one Bristol single-deck acquisition in this section.

Bristol

The coach fleet was considerably updated in 1954 with the arrival of 30 Bristol LS6Gs with ECW C38F bodies. These featured front roof lights with destination screens mounted below the windscreen, and inward-opening doors, all being SOL-inspired details which were subsequently offered by ECW to its Tilling clients. The rain splashers over the windows were removed some time after 1959. At least one of this batch of coaches was allocated to each depot, so they had provincial brown floral seating. *R H G Simpson*

All of the Bristol LS and MW coaches were downgraded to dual-purpose status between 1963 and 1965, being reseated to 40 (retaining 2+2 rear seating) or less commonly 41, but only some of those in the 1954 batch were eventually painted into bus livery as worn here by A26A. All 50 of the LSs moved to Edinburgh at this time to displace the overheating Reliances, and the considerable differences between this view and the one above are evident. *R H G Simpson*

FLEET	REG NOS	TYPE		YEAR	BODY
A1-30	LSC 61-90	LS6G	(30)	1954	ECW C38F
A31-50	NSG 793-812	LS6G	(20)	1956	ECW C38F
A622-641	RSC	MW6G	(20)	1958	ECW C38F
(All of the LS and MW coaches had Gardner 6HLW 112hp engines and 5-speed constant mesh gearboxes.)					
A162-94	EWS-D	RELH6G	(33)	1966	Alexander Y C38Ft
A195-206	EWS-D	RELH6G	(12)	1966	Alexander Y C45F
A272-9	LFS-F	REMH6G	(8)	1969	Alexander M C42Ft
A315-32	OSF-G	LH6P	(18)	1970	Alexander Y C38F
A333-48	SFS-H	LH6P	(16)	1970	Alexander Y C38F
A349-73	SFS-H	REMH6G	(25)	1970	Alexander M C42Ft
A374	SWG 678H	LH6P	(1)	1970	Alexander Y DP41F
Originally Midland, ex-Highland, 1971					

The 20 LS coaches delivered in 1956 were similar to the 1954 vehicles, but rather than being intended as provincial coaches, they featured the grey London seat colours and initially were allocated equally between Airdrie and Edinburgh. When A42A went through its first CoF in 1963, alongside the 1951 Regal IV London coaches (going through on their 12-year CoF), the latter were fitted with Dawson heaters, and the opportunity was taken to fit a similar heater to this bus, hence the grille. It remained unique - thank goodness.
R H G Simpson

All dolled up and ready to go! The final LS coach, A50H, without rain splashers over the windows, is ahead of an MW coach in St Enoch Square in Glasgow. The company's coaching activities also extended to Glasgow, and Airdrie depot often took a good proportion of the coach fleet when allocated new.
R H G Simpson

SOL returned to Bristol in 1958 for a further 20 coaches, but this time took the then new MW6G chassis, with ECW bodies. A622 was the very first MW coach to enter service and sister A638A is seen 'somewhere in England' beside a BET-style vehicle, as coach number 12 on the two-, three- or four-day Edinburgh to London service. These were the last coaches to be delivered without Scottish Omnibuses fleetnames, and had brown provincial seating moquette. *R H G Simpson*

The MWs were also relegated to semi-coach duties in 1963-5 and similar alterations to the LSs were effected, slam doors being retained. The destination screens were a fibreglass unit made at Marine Works. New Street depot only had ten of these. A640G is noted in 1965 on a private hire. ZA634A has been modelled in 1:76 scale by EFE. *R H G Simpson*

Following the six 1963 Reliances purchased for the London overnight service, the entire London fleet was replaced in 1966 following the purchase of 33 Bristol RELH6G coaches, the first with Alexander bodies. Because the London service only had peak demand on high days and holidays, they were often used on other duties and XA168A is inevitably on the Glasgow Express in St Andrew Square bus station. *Gavin Booth*

The front grilles on all Alexander bodied REs, and LHs, was an unusual but attractive design. A study of these is made in New Street depot when new, also depicting XA168, but this time before a depot code had been affixed. *Gavin Booth*

The final 12 RELHs came as C45F, with jack knife doors and these too were eventually relegated to dual-purpose duties, the jack-knife doors making this easier. YA195 is in a Cambridge road obviously affected by gales on its way to London on the three-day service. Why the company never went for further RELHs instead of Leopards will never be known.
Gavin Booth

The yellow and black and 'Scottish' blue liveries co-existed for a while, and pictured in New Street are XA361A, nearer the camera in yellow and black, and XA279A in blue and white. *Gavin Booth*

18 Bristol LH6Ps were ordered for 1969 delivery, with a further 16 for 1970, all with C38F coachwork, being the last coaches with 2+2 rear seating. The 1969 examples were delayed by a year, and both batches were built together in spring 1970. Along with the other 1969 vehicles YA323A retained its G suffix registration, making a mockery of the system. One of the reasons LHs were chosen rather than Bedfords was to ensure the driver could be heard when speaking on the microphone! Leyland engines were avoided. *Gavin Booth*

BRISTOL DOUBLE-DECKERS

FOLLOWING THE UPGRADING of the coach fleet in the early 1950s through rebodying and purchase of new vehicles, it became essential that the double-deck fleet was renewed, more especially so since the withdrawal of tram services both in Edinburgh and Glasgow resulted in considerably more work and extra loadings, coupled with the Suez crisis which resulted in a general reduction in frequencies, notably in the weekday mornings.

Demonstrator and prototype Lodekka LHY 949 was operated in service in 1950; later, LDL and FLF demonstrators would be operated. Some Scottish Bus Group companies took delivery of early Lodekkas - Western and Central operating numerous 1955 LD6Gs. But again the dual-sourcing policy came into effect, and it transpired that the only SBG fleet which was to standardise solely on the Lodekka was SMT. That is why numerous Leyland Titans and subsequently Albion Lowlanders and Daimler Fleetlines went into the Alexander, Western and Central fleets as well as Lodekkas. It is equally doubtful that Bristol/ECW would have had the capacity to build all the Lodekkas that the SBG might have wanted. The only exception to this was the appearance in 1957 of 20 Leyland PD2/20s (see under Leyland double-deckers) acquired in a desperate rush.

The SMT Lodekka fleet was characterised by the many detail differences within batches, some of which were unique to the company. These are covered in the attached tables. Bristol/ECW fans will pore over these for hours, but it never ceases to amaze me that the company management went to all the bother of specifying these alterations and differences even within batches. The company became a staunch user of the Cave-Browne-Cave heating system, and was the only SBG company to do so (apart from a few 1961 Lodekkas delivered to Central SMT). SMT had one of the largest Lodekka fleets in the country, operating every type of Lodekka apart from the FL model, even though the FSFs were acquired secondhand in 1977. For ease, all Lodekkas are shown in the attached lists, even if secondhand. The first production VRTs, and the only 33ft-long VRT buses bodied by ECW, were delivered to the fleet in 1968 (they ought to have been re-registered with G suffixes), followed by standard VRTs in 1969. It is common knowledge that these were exchanged for NBC FLFs in 1973 following mechanical difficulties which the SBG deemed fatal, although they gave excellent service in the south. Perhaps allocating 17 of them to Baillieston depot, the worst in the company, sealed their fate even before they entered service! At least AA287/8, 305/7 survived beyond the Millennium as psvs, the first two as open-toppers, the others with the independent Johnson of Hodthorpe. AA620 and AA971 are preserved, the latter as an open-topper which it became after normal service.

The first Lodekkas arrived in 1956, and AA13G was the only one to have the old-style grille, which was later removed. Some were painted in two-tone green and cream, but others were in light green and cream when new. AA1 and 2 were experimentally fitted with platform doors about three years after delivery. All had a full complement of opening windows - the only Lodekkas in the fleet to have so from new. Twelve went to Highland in 1963 - see the odds and ends chapter. All also featured lower deck rear windows, split in the narrow form. *Photobus*

Very unusually, SOL re-acquired some of its 1956 LDs from Highland for further service in 1971, but because it had reused the fleetnumbers with 1964 FS6Gs, they had to take new numbers upon purchase. AA580C (formerly AA11) stands in Baillieston. Note how the cream band has been extended round the front over the moulding - this being done from around 1967 onwards. With the 1977 vehicle shortage, these LDs went on for 22 years, this bus lasting until 1978. ZB964 is directly in front of the vehicle and a VRTLL6G beside it. *Gavin Booth*

No fewer than 40 LD6Gs came in 1957, and these had the updated style of ECW body. Note the alternate opening windows, deemed suitable after the 1956 experiments with Monocoaches, provided the front upper deck windows opened. SOL was persuaded to take one with Cave-Brown-Cave heating, and this was AA608A, thought to have been the first with both C-B-C heating and opening top deck front windows, previous LDs having fixed upper windows. Some Lodekkas with an identical upper deck arrangement were produced for Bristol around the same time. AA598H was fitted with platform doors in 1964 following a rear-end collision. *R H G Simpson*

LODEKKAS PURCHASED NEW

FLEET	REGN NOS.	TYPE	YEAR	BODY
AA1-15	NSG 778-92	LD6G (15)	1956	ECW H60R
(AA1/2 H60RD wef 1959)				
AA582-621	OWS	LD6G (40)	1957	ECW H60R
(AA598 H60RD wef 1964)				
AA642-57	RSC	LD6G (16)	1958	ECW H60R
AA719-49	SWS	LD6G (31)	1959	ECW H60R
(AA730-49 H60RD wef 1964)				
AA750-74	USC	LD6G (25)	1959/60	ECW H60RD
AA845-69	WSC	LD6G (25)	1961	ECW H60RD
AA870-94	YWS	FLF6G (25)	1962	ECW H70F
AA943-60	8943 SF etc	FS6G (18)	1963	ECW H60RD
AA11-21	AFS-B	FS6G (11)	1964	ECW H60RD
AA22-46	CSG-C	FLF6G (25)	1965	ECW H70F
AA207-31	GSG-D	FLF6G (25)	1966	ECW H76F
AA280-304	LFS-F	VRTLL6G (25)	1968	ECW H83F
AA305-14	OSF-G	VRTSL6G (10)	1969	ECW H77F

- 5-speed constant mesh gearboxes fitted to all 1956/7 vehicles. All other new Lodekkas 4 speed constant mesh
- 5-speed semi automatic gearboxes fitted to all VRTs
- All LD and FS models had Gardner 6LW 112bhp engines
- All FLFs and VRTs bought new had Gardner 6LX 150bhp engines
- Cave-Browne-Cave heating fitted to AA608, 762-74, 845-94, 943-60, 11-46
- New style radiator grilles fitted from AA883 onwards (May 1962)
- Cream window rubbers fitted from AA943 onwards
- AA887-94 (at least) and AA943-60 had illuminated advert panels
- AA37-46, 207-31 had internal screen changing equipment and no step built into the front grille

Far left: The 1958 intake comprised only 16 LDs, but they differed from the 1957 batch in only having four-speed gearboxes, the gap between third and fourth being considered too great for the busy hilly routes around Edinburgh, the majority of the five-speed LDs being transferred elsewhere as soon as practicable. AA644A comes down the Bridges on its way to St Andrew Square. Coupled with the 1957 deliveries, these brought to 56 the number of the updated ECW LD body with push-out upper deck hoppers delivered without platform doors! *R H G Simpson*

Right: Split-new in 1959 and without an allocation code, AA747 is off to Balerno, a commuting town that was then just outside the Edinburgh City boundary. The 1959 and 1960 LDs, also 56 in number, had the pull-in type of upper deck window hopper in line with ECW practice. *Photobus*

ACQUIRED LODEKKAS

FLEET	REGN NOS.	TYPE	BODY	ORIGIN
AA4, 6, 7	GCS 238/46/7	LD6G (3)	ECW H60R	Ex Western SMT, 1971. Cannibalised
AA5	GCS 245	LD6G (1)	ECW O60R	Ex Western SMT, 1971 as H60R
AA8/9	GCS 248/9	LD6G (2)	ECW H60R	Ex Western SMT, 1971
AA576-81	NSG 780-2/6/8/91	LD6G(6)	ECW H60R	Reacquired from Highland, 1971
AA965-72	KPM 85-92E	FLF6G (8)	ECW H70F	Ex Southdown (Brighton, Hove & District), 1973
AA973/4	LBL 847/8E	FLF6G (2)	ECW H70F	Ex Thames Valley & Aldershot, 1973
AA975-86	KVF 476-87F	FLF6G(12)	ECW H70F	Ex Eastern Counties, 1973
AA987-9	LAH 488-90E	FLF6G (3)	ECW H70F	Ex Eastern Counties, 1973
AA990/1	KDL 144/5F	FLF6G (2)	ECW H70F	Ex Southern Vectis, 1973
AA992-4	ONG 349/50/3F	FLF6G (3)	ECW H70F	Ex Eastern Counties, 1973
AA995-8	RHN 948-51F	FLF6G (4)	ECW H70F	Ex United, 1973
AA999	SHN 252F	FLF6G (1)	ECW H70F	Ex United, 1973
AA430/7/8/41/4/8	DGM	FSF6G (6)	ECW H60F	Ex Central SMT, 1977

- AA990/1 were the only FLFs in the fleet with Gardner 6LW engines, the rest having 6LX engines. All of the above acquisitions had 5-speed constant mesh gearboxes except Central SMT's FSFs (4-speed). It is thought that the company operated more secondhand Lodekkas than any other operator, apart from West Riding. Also, United Counties LRP 736E, an FLF6B, with Bristol BVW engine, was received in exchange for VRT AA286, presumably before the bonnet was opened up!

Although a further 25 LD6Gs appeared in late 1959/early 1960, there were two types delivered within the same batch. AA750-61 came without Cave-Brown-Cave heating, and were allocated principally to the west. Here AA759B is on the lengthy Glasgow-Edinburgh via Shotts service in pristine condition. The 1960 LDs were the final double-deckers to have green floral-pattern seats, and AA772 was reupholstered in 1965 with blue floral seats similar to AA46 (see page 46), but it was too costly to extend the scheme. *R H G Simpson*

Notwithstanding the introduction of the F series Lodekkas over a year beforehand, another 25 LD6Gs came in 1961, and these along with other SBG examples were the final LDs built. AA851 is in Glasgow clearly demonstrating the open mesh style of C-B-C grilles fitted to the first ten, AA855-69 having slatted covers! These had red bus seats and fluorescent lighting. The cream band continues round the front, and the bulkhead window also has a hopper, these features being peculiar to all C-B-C LDs and FSs in the fleet, apart from AA608. *R H G Simpson*

Just to prove the point, here is AA859A, a very late LD6G with slatted C-B-C covers, coming off duty on its way back to New Street depot followed on a similar exercise by LH6P, A327A. These Lodekkas gave excellent service and many were sorry to see their withdrawal, a considerable number after 20 years hard work. *John Burnett*

The very first FLF in the fleet was AA870C, one of 25 built in 1962, seen in Glasgow on the ex-Lowland route to Easterhouse which ran every five minutes. There were three variations within the batch, those up to AA882 having the traditional front grille, AA883 onwards being fitted with the new-style grille. Also AA887-94 had illuminated advert panels. Note the unusual opening window arrangement, unique to SOL for all of its new standard-length FLFs.

AA883-94 were the only FLFs built to feature new-style grilles, C-B-C heating and black window rubbers all on the same bus. *R H G Simpson*

For reasons unknown, but probably the accountants won the day, the 1963 Lodekkas were only FS6Gs, and AA946A rounds St Andrew Square off to the East Lothian county town of Haddington. The =Scottish= fleetname and the dark green mudguards show up well. All of the buses in this batch were identical.
R H G Simpson

There were subtle differences in the 1965 FLFs. AA25A (very quickly thereafter reallocated to Musselburgh) has nipped out in front of an Edinburgh Daimler CWG5 toiling up the hill into St Andrew Square. The lower deck front bulkhead window was fixed, but they otherwise were similar to AA883-86 apart from the cream window rubbers.
R H G Simpson

The final ten, AA37-46 had internal screen-changing equipment resulting in a centrally positioned registration number and no step to its right. Also, AA46A had numerous detail differences to the others - like the convex, rather than concave, tip to the upper cream band; ducting in the central band moved one bay back; sharper corners to the door intrusion into the central band; different panel mouldings at the rear; black mudguards which it retained throughout several repaints and blue floral pattern seats and panelling internally. If you cannot have blue outside the bus, you can inside! It is seen in Dunfermline with a Fife LD6G behind. *R H G Simpson*

Delivery of the 25 1966 FLFs was brought forward from 1967 by several months to co-incide with the opening of the new Dalkeith depot, and accordingly all were allocated there for all their lives, apart from a handful that went to Bathgate in their final year. They were the longer 76-seat design, and continued with the blue seat theme, but with a checked pattern and also had internal screen-changing equipment. The opening window arrangement has also been tidied up. In special 75 years commemorative livery, AA208G plies its trade to Rosewell to the south of Edinburgh. *John Burnett*

In November 1968 Eastern Scottish placed the first production Bristol VRTs to be built in service. The 25 long wheelbase chassis had handsome ECW 83-seat bodywork. Perhaps due to under-development at the design stage, initial teething troubles progressed to become chronic reliability problems. AA280 was photographed in Balerno on its first day in service. *Gavin Booth*

The following year saw another batch of ten VRTs arrive, but this time they were the standard wheelbase variant seating 77. These fared little if any better in terms of reliability and were part of the 1973 arrangement with NBC whereby Scottish Bus Group VRs were swapped on a one for one basis for late model Lodekka FLFs. AA313 was seen heading out of Glasgow on the long trunk route to Edinburgh. *Harry Hay*

Secondhand Lodekka purchases in 1971 came from Western SMT and these were numbered in the old series of original 1956 LDs, but did not duplicate the FS numbers. AA9C is on a typical Glasgow local operating from Baillieston. The cream band is moulded round the front, and again these buses gave many years' service to SOL.
Stewart J Brown

The 35 ex NBC FLFs were very conveniently numbered AA965-99, coming after Reliance B964. Ex-Eastern Counties example AA986A plods its way uphill towards Edinburgh from Penicuik. The fetish with opening windows continues - alternate hoppers being carefully fitted. All those with Tilling-style side-by-side destination screens were changed to standard SBG hexagonal pattern. Five-speed gearboxes made these popular vehicles. *John Burnett*

Those fitted with T-shape destination screens retained them, as the standard SBG blind just fitted, although when the NBC numbers required replacement small SBG number screens were used without blanking which made life confusing. While the majority of the ex-Brighton, Hove & District buses were allocated to Dalkeith depot, and were therefore kept in good condition, AA968C went to Baillieston and is noted in a typical Glasgow environment. *Photobus*

LEYLAND DOUBLE-DECKERS

PRIOR TO THE WAR Leyland was the principal double-deck provider, and a number of all-Leyland TD variant Titans were operated. It is fair to say, however, that the double-deck component in the fleet was never as pronounced prewar as for example in the late 1950/60s, the company preferring to run more frequent services with single-decks, with significant duplication.

One unfrozen TD5 was delivered during the war (since preserved in blue), and 18 prewar Tigers were rebuilt to TD5 standard and rebodied by Alexander, these previously having been London coaches. Although Leyland fell from favour, partly due to the SBG dual-sourcing policies, when the AEC Regent III and Bristol Lodekka reigned supreme, in 1957 20 PD2/20 Titans (chassis diverted from Edinburgh Corporation) with Park Royal lowbridge bodies were hurried into service from Airdrie depot for tram-replacement purposes, which seemed catch the company out, typically being out of touch with happenings in the west.

While some of the later Fleetlines were badged as Leylands, I have included them under Daimler (where they ought to be, and for clarity). Just before the 1985 split-up into Lowland, and casting off depots to Central, Midland and Kelvin, orders for ten Leyland Lion double-deckers were placed (with a further three coming in 1986), and most of these splendid rare machines still ply the streets today, having proved to be extremely reliable. The Leyland double-deckers acquired from Lowland Motorways and Baxter's are dealt with under their relative chapters. A number of early secondhand Leyland Titans came from other SBG companies, often running for some years for the company, and these are covered in the one-off chapter, whilst those from Lothian Region Transport can be found in the writings on the 1977 vehicle shortage.

The only deviation from Lodekka purchases were 20 Leyland PD2/20s with lowbridge Park Royal bodies on chassis apparently diverted from Edinburgh Corporation that appeared in 1957. Bought for tram replacement duties that caught SOL on the hop, all were allocated to Airdrie and moved to Baillieston depot when it opened in 1960. HH564 is seen in Glasgow. Over the years they were neglected by the depots, and systematically destroyed by the passengers as happened so often to SOL buses in the west. *R H G Simpson*

Twenty of the then new Olympian were delivered with stylish ECW bodies in 1982. HH113 (ULS 113X - registered in Stirlingshire due to lack of matching Edinburgh numbers). These buses were delivered before the withdrawal of the last Lodekkas. Note the opening upper deck front windows - all were delivered with these but they were removed within weeks after some structural problems! *John Burnett*

FLEET NOS	TYPE	YEAR	BODY
HH548-67 (OWS)	Titan PD2/20 (20)	1957	Park Royal L56R
HH96-115 (ULS-X)	Olympian ONLXB/1R (20)	1982	ECW H77F
HH116-35 (ALS-Y)	Olympian ONLXB/1R (20)	1983	Alexander H79F
LL136-43 (A-BSC)	Olympian ONLXB/1R (8)	1984	Alexander H79F
LL144/5 (B-GSC)	Olympian ONTL11/2R (2)	1984	Alexander CH63F
LL159-63 (B-KSC)	Olympian ONTL11/1R (5)	1985	Alexander H79F
LL174-83 (C-VSF)	Lion TL11 (10)	1986	Alexander DPH86F

Further Olympians came with Alexander R type bodies in 1983, 1984 and 1985, demonstrating yet again the difficulty Alexander had in producing a balanced lowheight design. LL142 stands ready for its next duty in Buchanan bus station in Glasgow when almost new in July 1984. *Harry L Barker*

Without doubt the most interesting double-deckers in the fleet were the Leyland Lions, ordered by the nationalised company prior to being split up into Lowland, Midland and Central. Ten came in 1986 and a further three in 1987 and all had this attractive style of Alexander R type bodywork with coach seats. They were the first R types to have the deep V windscreens, necessary because of the Lion's high driving position, but quickly adopted for other Alexander designs because they were practical and attractive. These rare beasts proved to be very reliable and all but one survived into the Millennium, many looking good for well over 15 years service. *John Burnett*

A pair of Alexander RLC bodied Leyland Olympian ONTL11/2R coaches arrived in 1984. It had been hoped that these could be used to solve capacity problems on some Citylink duties but they proved to be unreliable and uneconomical when used on express work. The total seating capacity was only 63, with only 20 seats downstairs. CLL144 was photgraphed leaving Buchanan bus station. *John Burnett*

LOWLAND MOTORWAYS

IT WAS CLEAR to the management of the SBG that it could best serve the public if a monopoly of services was created in its operating territory. Lowland Motorways worked a number of urban services in the area to the east of Glasgow city centre, it is fair to say with a motley (or if you are an enthusiast, superb) collection of vehicles adorned in a dull green and greyish green livery which included such gems as two ECW Beverley Bar Leyland TD5s from East Yorkshire, six Cravens-bodied RTs from London, and a unique PD2/20 built in 1955 but with a crash gearbox and E181 engine making it mechanically similar to a PD1, but with tin front. There was also an Albion CX19, two Daimler CWA6s (ex-Western SMT), and numerous TD4, TD5 and TD7s, many new to Plymouth Corporation and the erstwhile Greenock Motor Services, and one from Eastern National. The two Leyland Lowloaders, being Atlantean prototypes, were not included in the takeover.

On the single-deck side there were two prototype/demonstration Leyland Tiger Cubs, one of which H106 (LYS 943) went temporarily to Stark's of Dunbar in 1960 (amazingly a third prototype came to SOL with Stark's of Dunbar), a Royal Tiger, a Regal IV, two Regal I with rare Parr bodies ex-City of Oxford, and some Regal IIIs. Lowland was taken over on 13 January 1958 and while initially operations were continued using many of the vehicles from Airdrie (Clarkston) depot, it became necessary to open a new depot and modernise the fleet. In 1960 the new Baillieston depot opened for this purpose.

To many it is difficult to understand why Lowland came under the SOL umbrella; it was because of the Airdrie connections and SOL worked in from the east to Glasgow - but it could so easily have gone into the then Alexander empire which worked as Lawson's from Kirkintilloch, and with whom it would probably have sat more comfortably. When Lowland was purchased it operated 36 vehicles (26 double-deck, 10 coaches). It only ever purchased two new double-deckers - all-Leyland PD2/12s new in 1954 and which were moved eventually to Edinburgh and ran for many years there, adding further interest to the main fleet.

LOWLAND MOTORWAYS FLEET COMPOSITION AS ACQUIRED ON 13 JANUARY 1958

Fleet/Reg No.	Chassis	Body	Notes
B44 (JJF 604)	AEC Regal I 0662	Parr FC35F(1953)	New COMS 181, 1935
B45 (JJF 605)	AEC Regal I 0662	Parr FC35F (1953)	New COMS 159, 1936
B46 (GGA 524)	AEC Regal III 6821A	Duple C35F	New 12/48
B47 (GGG 785)	AEC Regal III 6821A	Duple C33F	New 4/50
B48/9 (HGE 796/7)	AEC Regal III 6821A	Burlingham FC33F	New 5/50
B50 (JGD 978)	AEC Regal IV 9821E	Burlingham C35C	New 7/51
BB1-6 (JXC 181,224/0 KGK 743/60/8)	AEC RT	Cravens H56R	New 1949 to LT as RT1422/61/57/84, 1501/9
EE1/2 (ASD 492/5)	Daimler CWA6	Brush L53R	New Western SMT, 1944
H105 (JGD 667)	Leyland PSU1/15	Burlingham C35C	New 5/51
H106 (LYS 943)	Leyland PSUC1/2	Alexander C41F	See note below
H107 (FCS 451)	Leyland PSUC1/2	Alexander C41F	Ex demonstrator
HH1 (FEV 181)	Leyland TD5	ECW L53R (1949)	New ENOC, 1937
HH2/3 (GAT 61/2)	Leyland TD5	ECW HBB54R (1948)	New EYMS, 1939
HH4 (CS 7024)	Leyland TD5	Leyland H56R	New Western SMT, 1938 Body rebuilt by ECW 1951
HH5 (LVA 484)	Leyland PD2/20 Spl	NCME L55R	See note below
HH6/7 (LYS 757/8)	Leyland PD2/12	Leyland L53R	New 1954
HH8/9 (JY 6759/66)	Leyland TD4	Weymann L48R	New Plymouth CT, 1936
HH10 (BDR 255)	Leyland TD5	Weymann L53R	New Plymouth CT, 1938
HH11-3 (CDR 352/3/7)	Leyland TD7	Roe L55R	New Plymouth CT, 1942
HH14/5 (VS 3066/7)	Leyland TD4	Leyland L53R	New Greenock MS, 1936
HH16/7 (VS 3636/40)	Leyland TD5	Leyland L53R	New Greenock MS. 1937
SS3 (DGB 470)	Albion CX19	Pickering H56R	Not believed used

Special Notes:

H106 (LYS 943) - Chassis number 520002. Prototype Tiger Cub built as PSUC1/1 bus model and used as experimental PSUC1/2 by shortening rear chassis frame to enable boot to be fitted in a coach thereby becoming a PSUC1/2. Sent to Stark's in 5/60 on loan (see Stark's chapter) where it worked alongside EWG 240, another prototype Tiger Cub with chassis 520003.

HH5 (LVA 484) - Although designated PD2/20, this was built by Leyland as an 'answer' to AEC's Regent V MD3RV lightweight model and had an E181 engine and constant mesh gearbox - effectively a PD1 in a PD2 27ft x 8ft tin front frame. It remained unique and started life with Hutchison, Overtown where it was quickly disposed of after a few weeks.

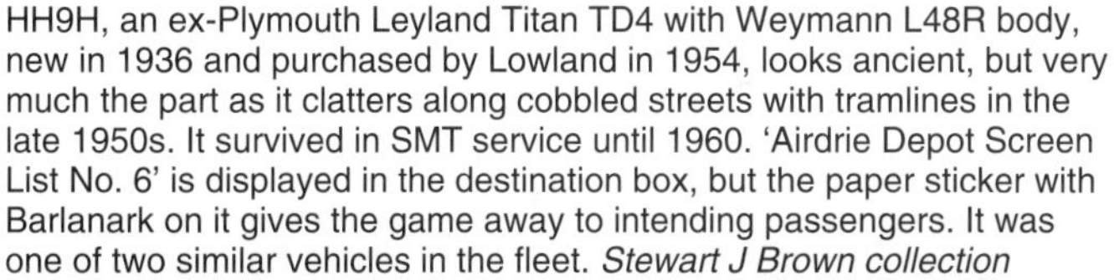

HH9H, an ex-Plymouth Leyland Titan TD4 with Weymann L48R body, new in 1936 and purchased by Lowland in 1954, looks ancient, but very much the part as it clatters along cobbled streets with tramlines in the late 1950s. It survived in SMT service until 1960. 'Airdrie Depot Screen List No. 6' is displayed in the destination box, but the paper sticker with Barlanark on it gives the game away to intending passengers. It was one of two similar vehicles in the fleet. *Stewart J Brown collection*

Three Roe L55R wartime TD7s also came from Plymouth in 1954 via Millburn Motors, and HH12H is seen in this 1958 shot also off to Barlanark, but this time passing a stop, presumably with a full load, leaving a number of frustrated passengers behind! The bus did not survive for even a year with SMT, but its sisters HH11 and HH13 were taken off in 1960 and 1959 respectively. *Photobus*

Originally new to Greenock Motor Services, HH14H was one of four Titans to come from that company (albeit via Western SMT), from two batches. This 1936 all-Leyland TD4 had an L53R body and was withdrawn in 1959 - it too has the screen list number 6 destination! *Photobus*

HH1H was new to Eastern National as its no.3712 in 1937, and was rebodied by ECW in 1949 as L53R. It passed via United Counties to Lowland in 1957. One of the first Lowland vehicles to be withdrawn, it was only in Glasgow in both Lowland and SMT ownership for about a year - so this is indeed a rare photograph. *Photobus*

Amongst the various vehicles taken over from Lowland were two Daimler CWA6s with utility Brush L53R bodies which were new in 1944 to Western SMT. They proved to be the only front-engined Daimler double-deckers ever operated by the company, and here EE2H awaits its next duty in a typical Glasgow scene. It was withdrawn in 1959, its sister in 1960. *Photobus*

In response to AEC's mediumweight Regent V chassis, Leyland produced a prototype for a competing vehicle, and here it is. Although officially designated as a PD2/20, in fact HH5 had an E181 engine and constant mesh gearbox as found in the PD1, albeit within 27ft by 8ft frames and a tin front. Exhibited at the 1955 Scottish Show, and delivered to Hutchison of Overtown, it was very quickly snapped up by Lowland. Eventually moved to Edinburgh it, and its Northern Counties body, added yet more variety to the New Street allocation. It was taken off in 1967, not being put through its second CoF. *Photobus*

Lowland also had an interesting collection of single-deckers, and heading the line up of no fewer than six buses is B46H, a 1948 Duple C35F-bodied Regal III, complete with paper stickers. Taken out of service in 1962, behind it is an SOL Monocoach, followed by some Central SMT Titans, both Leyland- and Northern Counties-bodied examples. *Photobus*

Right: Lowland also provided six ex-London Cravens-bodied RTs, all new in 1949. BB2H is in Glasgow displaying its light green and cream very well. Unfortunately these buses had relatively short lives, BB2 going in 1964, the remainder in 1963. SOL's own Regent IIIs lasted for almost 20 years. *Stewart J Brown collection*

Below: Nothing was ever straightforward with Lowland, and two ex-City of Oxford Regal Is were rebodied with rare Parr of Leicester FC35F bodies in 1953 when 'only' 18 years old. B45H is incredibly on the trunk Edinburgh-Glasgow express service despite the chassis being well over 25 years old when this shot was taken in 1961! The coach was to last for another year. *Gavin Booth*

Below right: Purchased new by Lowland in 1950 were two Burlingham FC33F-bodied AEC Regal IIIs - the newest Regal IIIs in the fleet - and one might have expected that being almost standard they would have lasted beyond 1962, but they were never given their 12-year CoF. B49H is on a Shettleston local service. *Photobus*

Ex-East Yorkshire no.376 was a Leyland TD5, rebodied with Beverley Bar roof by ECW in 1948 to an H54R layout. One of two in the fleet, these had the longest lives of the secondhand Lowland double-deckers and survived well into 1962, being replaced by Bristol FLFs at Baillieston. A Park Royal Leyland PD2/20 stands next to it. *Photobus*

Lowland purchased two Burlingham-bodied coaches, both Seagulls on underfloor-engined chassis. One, B50H, is seen on a hire and represents what might have been had SOL's own Regal IVs been bodied by Burlingham. The other was a Royal Tiger, H105 with similar body, both C35C. The Regal was another example of rare fleet renumbering, becoming B36 in 1964 to make way for new Reliances. *Photobus*

The only new double-deckers purchased by Lowland were two all-Leyland PD2/12s in 1954 with lowbridge 55-seat bodywork. HH7A, along with its sister HH6, moved to Edinburgh after a few years where they intermingled with Regent IIIs, Lodekkas and ex-Baxter's Regents, Bridgemasters, a Renown and other sundry buses to add even more interest to the fleet. It is parked sunbathing outside Musselburgh depot bound for the author's home village. *Photobus*

Light Green

A very early colour photo, taken in the days when SMT services departed from the centre of St Andrew Square in Edinburgh, showing two of the AEC Regent III with 53-seat lowbridge bodies bought in 1949/50. BB87, at the front, has a Burlingham body, and the bus behind has a Duple body. Both have the early non-diamond SMT fleetnames. *C Carter*

Roaring out of St Andrew Square bus station in September 1958, E22, a 1945 Guy Arab II 6LW with lowbridge Weymann body passes the stone frontage that had to be built as a concession to the architectural merit of the square. This bus passed to Highland later that year. *Gavin Booth collection*

Fifteen 1948 AEC Regal III were lengthened to 30ft and rebodied by Dickinson in 1953 with bodies that bore the characteristics of both Alexander and Burlingham. B332 on platform D at St Andrew Square bus station. *Photobus*

The 20 1957 Leyland PD2/20s with 56-seat lowbridge Park Royal bodies spent most of their lives in the west of Scotland. A careworn HH554 is seen in Glasgow in full light green SMT livery. *Photobus/R L Wilson / OTA*

On Tour

At the head of a line of Eastern Scottish coaches in Edinburgh's George Square in June 1975, YH424, a 1972 Leyland Leopard PSU3/3R with 45-seat Alexander Y type body, awaits conference delegates for a tour to Hopetoun House and The Forth Bridges. *Gavin Booth*

Eastern's tour departure point was on Platform E of St Andrew Square bus station, where YC568, a 1974 Bedford YRQ with 38-seat Alexander Y type body awaits its passengers. *Gavin Booth*

Returning from a day tour in 1985, YL332, a 1984 Leyland Tiger TRCTL11/2RH with 49-seat Plaxton Paramount body, in Princes Street, Edinburgh. The coach livery at this time used two shades of green. *Gavin Booth*

YL353, a 1987 Leyland Tiger TRCL10/3RZA with Duple 340 53-seat body, heads past the National Portrait Gallery in Edinburgh's Queen Street in 1988, towards the bus station. *John Burnett*

M Types

Awaiting its passengers on Platform E, 1969 Bristol REMH6G XA274 with 42-seat Alexander M type bodywork still wears the original yellow/black livery.
Gavin Booth

In 1976 the blue/white corporate SCOTTISH livery was introduced for SBG's Scotland-London services. The first coach to carry these colours, XA364, a 1970 Bristol REMH6G/Alexander M type, leaves St Andrew Square on the very first journey of a coach in these colours. Sadly, it broke down en route.
Gavin Booth

The last M type bodies for Eastern Scottish were mounted on six Seddon Pennine VII delivered in 1976. These were delivered in the blue/white livery and had six-speed manual gearboxes. These were the only examples of this chassis/body combination. XS749 is seen in 1979.
Harry Hay

Bristol Lodekkas

On the last stage of its journey from Haddington, AA867, a 1961 Bristol Lodekka LD6G with ECW 60-seat body, in Picardy Place heading towards St Andrew Square bus station. *Harry Hay*

In this atmospheric shot, AA39 passes along the cobbles of Market Street having been diverted from its normal route to Birkenside. *Gavin Booth*

In the famous SBG/NBC swap of VRTs for Lodekkas, Eastern received FLF6Gs from various NBC companies. AA965, still with Tilling-style destination display, sets out for Mayfield in May 1980. It was new to Brighton Hove & District in 1967 and passed to Eastern in 1973. *John Burnett*

Turning from Castle Street into Princes Street in May 1980, AA998 was new in 1968 to United Auto, and has been rebuilt with SBG-style destination display. *John Burnett*

Classic Halfcabs

Splashing through the snow at Sighthill in the 1960s, BB51, a 1948 AEC Regent III with severe-looking Alexander 53-seat lowbridge bodywork. *John Burnett*

In the spring of 1966, BB87 climbs out of Colinton on the 53 service to Balerno. It is a 1950 AEC Regent III with 53-seat lowbridge Burlingham body. *John Burnett*

The two 1957 AEC Regent V with Massey bodies that were acquired from Baxter's in 1962 passed to Alexander (Northern) in 1974. The former BB20 is seen at Aberdeen as NRC28, still in Eastern's green/cream. *John Burnett collection*

The Leyland Titans acquired from Baxter's included four rare Massey-bodied forward entrance lowbridge examples. HH45, a 1961 PD2/37, leaves St Andrew Square bus station for Haddington in April 1973, when day return fares on Eastern's Edinburgh-Glasgow service were 50p. *Gavin Booth*

Baxter's & Stark's

Delivered to Baxter's in 1962, but never used, this bus first entered service with SOL in green/cream as B964. It was transferred to Victoria depot in 1973 and painted in Baxter's colours, as seen here on an enthusiast tour at Airdrie in the mid-1970s. *Harry Hay*

Wearing Baxter's colours in October 1976 are DD694, a 1975 Daimler Fleetline CRG6LXB with 75-seat ECW body, and DD80, the 1965 Fleetline/Alexander. DD694 was delivered new in Baxter livery, while DD80, diverted from a Western SMT order, was the replacement for the burnt-out 9961 SF, which was subsequently rebodied. *Gavin Booth*

The highest number in the Eastern Scottish fleet was carried by AA999, a 1968 Bristol Lodekka FLF6G, a former United vehicle acquired via Northern General in exchange for a Bristol VRT. It is seen at Victoria depot in October 1976. *Harry Hay*

Turning into Quality Street, North Berwick, B908, a 1962 AEC Reliance 2MU3RA with Alexander 41-seat body, in Stark's colours, was one of four similar buses transferred from the main Eastern Scottish fleet in 1967. *Gavin Booth*

B66, a 1964 AEC Reliance 4MU3RA with 49-seat Alexander Y type body, sits in Elder Street, Edinburgh, waiting its turn to move into Platform D on a Pencaitland journey in 1978. It carries the light green Stark's colours and S depot code. *Harry Hay*

Y Types

Among the large intake of 56 Alexander Y type-bodied AEC Reliances in 1964 there were 12 with 49-seat dual-purpose bodies, like ZB73, seen in the Borders heading for Galashiels. *John Burnett*

The Seddon Pennine VII was designed for the Scottish Bus Group, and Eastern Scottish took the prototype as its no.ZS661. It is seen here when new in Lasswade. It carries an Alexander Y type 49-seat body and was new in 1973. *Gavin Booth collection*

A325 is one of the 1970 batch of Bristol LH, delivered as 38-seat coaches, but converted to B45F along with all of the 1969 buses. A few of the 1970 vehicles were simply repainted into dual-purpose livery and not reseated, and most of these went to the old Stark's operation. It is pictured in Galashiels. *John Burnett*

The only 53-seat Leyland Leopard/Alexander Y types delivered to Eastern Scottish were 10 PSU3/3R examples delivered in 1974. H557 is seen in Shandwick Place, Edinburgh, when new; all 10 were transferred to Central SMT in 1975. *Gavin Booth*

Photographed on delivery from Alexander's Falkirk coachworks in March 1980, Seddon Pennine VII/Y type S605 turns from Princes Street on to Waverley Bridge, en route for New Street depot. It is one of 40 53-seat buses delivered that year. *Gavin Booth*

In The Borders

B775, based at Galashiels depot, on a pleasant Border road in 1968. It is one of 35 AEC Reliance 2MU3RV with 41-seat Alexander bodies delivered in 1960. *John Burnett*

Sitting in the SOL depot in Berwick-upon-Tweed in the mid-1960s, B380, a 1949 AEC Regal III with Burlingham body, wearing the Lothian green colour with SMT diamond fleetname. *Photobus / R L Wilson / OTA*

The first generation of Border Courier vehicles were five Bedford CFL with Reeve Burgess 13-seat bodies with a goods compartment at the rear. ZC5 is seen when new. *Gavin Booth*

Leaving Galashiels on the trunk 62 service to Edinburgh, Peebles-based C737, a 1975 Bedford YRT with Alexander Y type 53-seat bus body.
Harry L Barker

Bedfords

While other SBG companies favoured Fords for their lighter-weight vehicles, Eastern preferred Bedfords. C232, the first of 20 delivered in 1967, is a VAM5 with Alexander 45-seat body. It is seen in Berwick on a local service in the spring of 1970. *Harry Hay*

Near the Ratho Park golf club in September 1980, C574, a 1974 Bedford YRQ with Alexander Y type body, on the 37 service to Ratho. *John Burnett*

When delivered in 1975, ZC729 carried the wrong registration, as seen here on a City Sightseeing tour in Edinburgh's Holyrood Park. A YRT with 49-seat Alexander body, it should show *MSF* 729P. The same vehicle, properly registered, in 1980, demonstrates why lowfloor buses have become popular with older passengers. *Gavin Booth/Harry L Barker*

SMT Red

Some of the Bristol Lodekka FLF6G received from NBC companies in exchange for Eastern Scottish VRTs ran in their NBC liveries for a short time with Eastern fleetnumbers. AA988, a 1967 ex-Eastern Counties vehicle, leaves St Andrew Square for Dunbar in 1973, with a fine selection of paper stickers. *Gavin Booth*

Another former Eastern Counties FLF, AA992, leaves the bus station on the 16 service in 1973. It was new in 1968 and carries the Tilling style of Eastern Counties livery. *Gavin Booth*

Central SMT's 1971 batch of ECW-bodied Daimler Fleetlines were soon transferred to other SBG companies, Eastern receiving 20 in 1975/6. Eastern's DD299 was one of 10 transferred to Highland Scottish in 1983, and is seen in Market Street, Edinburgh, repainted before transfer north. With the red brick mass of New Street depot in the background. *John Burnett*

Still wearing its Fife Scottish red/cream livery in 1986, DD490, a 1971 Daimler Fleetline/ECW, is seen in Bathgate after transfer from Fife. Transferred in 1986, it was withdrawn in 1987. *John Burnett*

Odd Colours

Unusual transfers from Central Scottish in 1986 were three 1981 Dennis Dominators with Alexander RL bodies. EE58 is seen on the Livingston circle late in 1986, wearing a unique variation of the two shades of green/cream livery. These buses, which had Rolls-Royce engines, were quickly transferred to Clydeside Scottish. *John Burnett*

Facing competition from Harris, Armadale, on a local route into Bathgate, Eastern Scottish repainted S850, a 1978 Seddon Pennine VII/Alexander Y type, in a colour scheme similar to that worn by Harris. It is seen in Bathgate. *John Burnett*

Another unusual livery on the Livingston circle, DD739, a former West Midlands PTE 1973 Daimler Fleetline CRG6LX with Park Royal 76-seat body, one of six borrowed from Ensign, Purfleet, for a few months late in 1986. *John Burnett*

More Dennis Dominators were acquired by Eastern in 1994, four former Leicester CityBus examples. EE226, with Marshall 76-seat body, and EE285 with East Lancs 76-seat body, are seen at the short-lived Centrex depot at Livingston in 1995, still in Leicester colours. They returned to Leicester CityBus. *John Burnett*

Van Hool Ailsas

The company took the opportunity in 1985 to purchase 25 Volvo Ailsas with unusual dual doored bodywork built in Ireland by Van Hool McArdle from South Yorkshire PTE. They were usually employed on the post deregulation network of routes in Edinburgh. VV5 (above) is seen on the short-lived route C4 through Comely Bank, while VV14 (above right) heads for genteel Morningside on the busy 23 service.

The original livery application used more dark green and used "Edinburgh Citybus" as a halfhearted attempt to establish a brand; VV20 (right) is seen at the top of Leith Walk in the summer of 1989.

The brisk performance and modern good looks, together with their musical back axles, ensured the popularity of these buses, VV4 (below) heads along Balcarres Street for the southern terminus of the C23.
Gavin Booth and John Burnett

Express

The first batch of Alexander-bodied Leyland Tigers had been ordered with Y type bodies but this was changed to the more versatile T type, some of these were liveried to promote the increasingly popular motorway express service X14 between Edinburgh and Glasgow. *Gavin Booth*

In each of the years 1981, 1982 and 1983 Duple-bodied Leyland Tigers were delivered; their powerful turbocharged engines provided the performance increase that was needed by this time. The body design clearly shows the influence of the earlier Alexander M type. *John Burnett*

Below, left: To provide increased capacity some of the Leyland Lions were redeployed on Citylink duties, this is CLL186 at the end of its long run from Edinburgh to Kilmarnock. *Harry Hay*

Above: This attractive livery, designed by Ray Stenning, was devised for SBG's Clansman Monarch package holiday business and worn by Eastern Scottish coaches used on this work. The colour scheme was later used by the privatised company as its coach hire livery. CL346, a 1987 Leyland Tiger/Duple 340, wears Clansman Monarch colours in Princes Street working on the Scottish Citylink 500 service. This was one of the last new vehicles supplied to Eastern under SBG control. *John Burnett*

An urgent need to increase the coach fleet in the early nineties resulted in some secondhand purchases; this Van Hool-bodied DAF came from Landtourer Coaches of Farnham. *John Burnett*

On Hire

The first Dennis Darts were fitted with Duple bodies, as both companies were part of the Hestair Group. This early example was tried in the Bathgate area in early 1990. *John Burnett*

By 1992 Duple had ceased production and Darts were available with other makers' bodies. A Plaxton-bodied 28-seater from the London United fleet was tried on city routes. *John Burnett*

When looking for a replacement for the Fleetline chassis, the company considered the Dominator; this East Lancs-bodied example from Leicester City Transport was loaned by Dennis and operated on the Edinburgh to Port Seton service in early 1981. *Gavin Booth*

Having purchased quantities of van-derived Dodge chassis and established the need for a small bus element in the fleet, the MCW Metrorider was tried in 1988. Although more Dodges were purchased the Metrorider subsequently became the standard small bus in the fleet during the early nineties by which time manufacture had transferred to Optare. *John Burnett*

The Alexander bodied Volvo B10Bs purchased in 1993 clearly failed to impress; two years later ten Optare Prisma Mercedes Benz 0405 were purchased. Optare's demonstrator was photographed in Armadale, note the SMT logo. *John Burnett*

In Preservation

Sadly, none of the SMT Regals survived into preservation. However a former Alexander example of the type joined the fleet in 1986; it was numbered B23 and was employed on special duties in the prewar 'Coronation' livery. Subsequently it was repainted in postwar light green and later returned to private ownership; it is kept at the Scottish Vintage Bus Museum at Lathalmond. *John Burnett*

AA620 has survived to represent the large fleet of LD Lodekkas. Although it looked smart when photographed in 1987 it has subsequently benefited from a considerable amount of restoration work. *John Burnett*

The number of former SMT buses in preservation has increased in recent years. The Lathalmond open weekend in 2003 featured this line up: ZS928, Seddon T type; XS750, Seddon M type; Lowland 856, Bristol VR/ECW; B91, AEC Reliance Y type 53-seat bus; Ailsa VV773 and B671, Reliance 38-seat coach. The bodywork on all except the Bristol is by Alexander. *John Burnett*

BAXTER'S OF AIRDRIE

ON 1 DECEMBER 1962 the well-loved independent Baxter's of Airdrie was taken over. Baxter's was a different kettle of fish from Lowland Motorways. Its fleet was modern and in good heart, being well maintained and tidy. The two-tone blue livery with grey relief was a well-respected sight in the Airdrie and Coatbridge areas, the company running the major share of local services, whereas SOL operated out-of-town routes from Airdrie, with Alexanders/Midland doing the same from Coatbridge.

On acquisition Baxter's operated 52 vehicles (25 double-deckers, 23 single buses/dual-purpose, and four coaches). The company had latterly standardised on exposed radiator Leyland Titans and 22 of the double-deckers were of varying types of Titan, all apart from two acquired Leyland-bodied examples having attractive lowbridge Massey bodies (four being forward entrance). Two Regent V MD3RVs, also with Massey bodies, and a Bridgemaster made up the remainder. The single-deck fleet comprised one AEC Regal III, two all-Leyland Royal Tiger buses, one Bedford SB, and an errant Tiger Cub all the rest being Reliances thereby fitting in well to the SOL fleet.

SOL thought it had no more to do than start painting Baxter's buses into fleet livery. It had been aware that the locals valued the Baxter name and wanted to be able to tell from a distance a Baxter bus from an SMT, and on painting the buses light green (but in a different style from the main fleet, roofs being green, and windows cream) it considered it had done enough to assuage local fears. In fact, partly because the Edinburgh management was well out of touch with local conditions in Airdrie and Coatbridge, it had totally misjudged the value of Baxter's goodwill in the community. There was considerable local press disquiet, and after a short period of only a few months, Baxter livery was reintroduced to the fleet. With inter-fleet and inter-depot transfers, this produced some remarkable sights - for example, Bristol LDs and FLFs in full Baxter livery.

Three Baxter buses on order at the time of take-over were placed into service in the main fleet, and their story is told in the captions. Baxter's Victoria depot survived for many years after acquisition, SOL thereby maintaining two depots in Airdrie with around 130-plus buses allocated to the town. Both depots have now closed. For a considerable period, buses carried two fleetnumbers - the official SOL number on one side of the bus, and Baxter's number on the other!

Baxter's had a modern fleet when acquired in 1962, the oldest double-deckers being two 1950 PD2/10s with Leyland L53R bodies acquired from Golden Eagle, Salsburgh. Seen resplendent in light green livery, HH29V is one of many that ultimately migrated to the Edinburgh area prior to withdrawal, although in this case for a more permanent stay to cover for Lodekkas transferred to Highland prior to delivery of the 1963 FS6Gs. It is noted in Platform E of St Andrew Square bus station bound for Balerno via Colinton. *Harry Hay*

Massey-bodied Leyland Titans had become Baxter's standard double-deckers in the mid to late 1950s and typifying the breed is HH33V, another PD2/10 of late 1956 with L55R body. It is seen in 1964 with the Baxter version of the light green livery, ie with a green roof to enable identification of an ex-Baxter bus to passengers. *Stewart J Brown*

In 1957 Baxter's tried out the AEC Regent V, and two Massey-bodied examples arrived, being of the MD3RV chassis type, ie mediumweight with AV470 engine. Both were very quickly moved to Edinburgh, and here BB20A is on the Bridges in Edinburgh. *John Burnett*

BAXTER'S BUS SERVICE, AIRDRIE
FLEET COMPOSITION AS ACQUIRED IN DECEMBER 1962

Fleet	Regn No.	Chassis	Body	New	To Main Fleet
B12	KVA 750	Crossley Reliance CMU3RV	Crossley B44F	1954	
B13	LVA 623	AEC Reliance MU3RV	Park Royal B45F	1955	11.66
B14	LVA 624	AEC Reliance MU3RV	Park Royal DP41F	1955	11.66
B15	LVD 218	AEC Reliance MU3RV	Alexander DP41F	1956	9.64
B16	LVD 219	AEC Reliance MU3RV	Alexander B45F	1956	
B17	NVA 142	AEC Reliance MU3RV	Alexander B45F	1956	10.67
B18	EVJ 807	AEC Regal I 0662	Massey B35F	See below	
B19,20	OVD 108/9	AEC Reliance MU3RV	Burlingham B45F	1957	10.67,12.67
B21/2	RVA 110/1	AEC Reliance MU3RV	Burlingham B45F	1958	12.67
B23	RVD 112	AEC Reliance MU3RV	Alexander DP41F	1958	
B24	SVD 114	AEC Reliance 2MU3RV	Burlingham B45F	1958	1.72
B25	UVA 115	AEC Reliance 2MU3RV	Burlingham B45F	1959	1.72
B26	UVA 116	AEC Reliance 2MU3RV	Burlingham DP41F	1959	8.67
B27	WVA 40	AEC Reliance 2MU3RV	Duple C41F	1960	
B28/9	WVD 117/8	AEC Reliance 2MU3RV	Alexander B45F	1960	
B30/1	119/20 AVA	AEC Reliance 2MU3RV	Alexander DP41F	1961	
B32	141 AVA	AEC Reliance 2MU3RV	Burlingham C41F	1961	
B33	42 CVD	AEC Reliance 2MU3RV	Plaxton C41F	1962	
B34	122 CVD	AEC Reliance 2MU3RV	Alexander B45F	1962	
BB18	78 BVD	AEC Bridgemaster 2B3RA	Park Royal H72F	1961	12.62
BB19,20	PVD 567/8	AEC Regent V MD3RV	Massey L55R	1957	12.62
C21	TVD 649	Bedford SB1	Burlingham C37F	1959	
H1	HVA 883	Leyland Royal Tiger PSU1/13	Leyland B44F	1953	10.67
H2	NTJ 985	Leyland Royal Tiger PSU1/17	Leyland B44F	See below	
H3	SVD 113	Leyland Tiger Cub PSUC1/2	Alexander DP41F	1958	
HH24/5	HVD 59,60	Leyland Titan PD2/10	Leyland L55R	1953	
HH26/7	KVA 657/8	Leyland Titan PD2/10	Massey L55R	1954	
HH28	KVD 286	Leyland Titan PD2/10	Massey L55R	1955	
HH29,30	FVD 224/5	Leyland Titan PD2/10	Leyland L53R	1950	4.63
HH31-3	NVD 861-3	Leyland Titan PD2/10	Massey L55R	1956	
HH34-6	OVA 864-6	Leyland Titan PD2/12	Massey L55R	1957	
HH37	RVD 469	Leyland Titan PD2/40	Massey L55R	1958	
HH38/9	TVA 70/1	Leyland Titan PD2/41	Massey L55R	1959	
HH40/1	TVD 72/3	Leyland Titan PD2/41	Massey L55R	1959	
HH42	VVD 74	Leyland Titan PD2/37	Massey L56F	1960	
HH43	WVA 75	Leyland Titan PD2/37	Massey L56F	1960	
HH44	XVA 276	Leyland Titan PD2/37	Massey L56F	1960	
HH45	YVD 77	Leyland Titan PD2/37	Massey L56F	1961	

Notes

- B18: EVJ 807 new to Jones, Burley Gate 1947 with Santus C33F body
- H2: NTJ 985 new 1952 to Corless, Coppull and acquired 1957
- H3: SVD 113 to Alexander Midland as MPD265 in 4/63 swapped with its MAC145 to become B35 (KWG 569) in SOL fleet - see Stark's section for background
- HH29, 30: FVD 224/5 new to Golden Eagle, Salsburgh
  A number of Leyland Titans also migrated to Edinburgh shortly before their withdrawal, but were repainted and used for a short period over summer months to overcome vehicle shortages. These short-term transfers are not noted above.

On take over:

- Baxter's 121 (121 CVD) was stored unused and became SOL B964
- Baxter's 79/80 (479/80 DVA) AEC Bridgemasters were virtually built - see AEC Double-deckers

After take over:

- The only NEW buses ever to be delivered to Baxter's in Baxter livery were ZB160/1, ZH476/7, DD80, 692-4
- B26 was the only bus in the fleet to work in all of Baxter's, Eastern Scottish Lothian Green and Stark's livery, although B25 also went to Stark's in Stark's livery in 5.72, and C21 to Stark's in 5.64

There were not that many secondhand vehicles in the Baxter's fleet, but one was B18, a 1947 Regal I that started life with a Santus C33F body, but was rebodied by Massey as B35F. Seen in New Street after withdrawal in June 1965, it is being painted into the obligatory grey before sale. It was lucky, because it went to a showman at Anstruther for a further lease of life. *Gavin Booth*

Later in life, and in dark green livery after transfer to New Street, B13 was photographed in St Andrew Square bound for Pencaitland. This had a high-speed rear axle and as such was popular among drivers who preferred this to a bus-geared Park Royal Monocoach. The winged emblem, also found on Monocoaches, is a direct result of Bill Shirley moving from ECW to Park Royal and taking this idea (from ECW on LSs) with him. *Photobus*

A return to Alexander bodies for buses resulted in the unusual sight of bus seats in this style of body, normally associated with SBG semi-coaches. B28V is working a private journey displaying its two-tone blue and grey livery. This bus, and sister, B29V, remained at Baxter's until withdrawal in 1975. *R H G Simpson*

An unusual coach for Baxter's was its no.49, which became SOL's C21. Seen as a true Baxter vehicle, it was moved directly to Stark's in May 1964, the only bus to have served in both ancillary fleets and not the main fleet. (B26, a 1959 Reliance, was the only bus to have served in all three!). It is a 1959 Bedford SB1 with Burlingham C37F coachwork.
R H G Simpson

While Baxter buses came east to Edinburgh, New Street-allocated vehicles went the other way for driver-only working including some Y type Reliances which New Street regarded as top link machines. B923V, seen as Baxter's no.923, a 1963 Reliance 2MU3RA with 41-seat dual-purpose body, works a Baxter's Coatbridge local in two-tone blue livery in 1969.
Stewart J Brown

Somewhat ironically, the very last two of hundreds of AEC Reliances delivered to SOL went to Baxter's rather than the main fleet. Baxter's no.160 is on an Omnibus Society tour and shows off its elegant lines to good effect. It is a 1966 Reliance 590 with 49 seat Y type bodywork.
Stewart J Brown

STARK'S OF DUNBAR

CONTINUING WITH THE COMPANY'S insatiable appetite to expand, the 14-vehicle fleet of Stark's of Dunbar was acquired on 1 January 1964. All were single-deckers, but were fairly mixed with one Bedford OB (with Ford 4D engine), four Ford Thames 570E coaches (which were quickly sold to Highland in exchange for some new Reliance coaches), one Leyland PS1, one Royal Tiger coach, two Reliances with standard Alexander bodywork, four Tiger Cubs (including the second prototype dating from 1952) and a Trojan.

This was an important acquisition as there was no depot to the east of Edinburgh between Musselburgh and Berwick-upon-Tweed, some 50 miles away, and the route network in East Lothian reflected this with virtually all services radiating from Edinburgh on a west-east basis, cross-country connections being poor, and in the hands of independents such as Stark's, Glass of Haddington and Wiles of Port Seton, with Armstrong's of Ormiston and Dunsmuir of Tranent running a number of contracts.

In addition to the local East Lothian routes, Stark's operated into Edinburgh on the trunk 30-mile long Edinburgh-Dunbar service which ran half-hourly and was part of the substantial Edinburgh-Newcastle group jointly worked by SMT and United. Therefore the buses of three operators could be seen on this service, and over the years standard United Bristol Ls, LSs, MWs and REs intermingled with Stark's fleet along with anything that SMT could muster, from Regent IIIs, Lodekkas to Reliances and Monocoaches and Bedfords. In a bid to avoid complete confusion to the passenger, there was an agreement that Stark's vehicles used on this service would carry the SMT diamond fleetname, and from the mid-1950s a livery which was specifically the opposite of SOL's - that is light green roofs and waistband, the remainder being cream. Stark's green was lighter than SMT's, but it had used two shades of green with no cream relief, and B39/40 first appeared in a cream and dark green livery in 1955.

After the takeover, however, in an effort to avoid the bad publicity which occurred after the Baxter situation, Stark's livery was retained, albeit in slightly altered layout (green above waistband, cream below) and all buses received the Stark's fleetname. This meant that those vehicles on the Dunbar service which had SMT fleetnames when owned and operated by Stark's, had Stark's fleetnames when owned by SMT! Stark's also had a depot at North Berwick which still exists today with increased responsibilities under the First Edinburgh banner. The Dunbar depot was sold to a supermarket chain. Stark's livery was retained for 15 years after take over, with the name continuing to appear over the North Berwick depot entrance until 1983.

One of the fascinating aspects of Stark's vehicle policy while independent was its apparent alliance with the Alexander empire, many of its new vehicles being identical to Alexander's, right down to seat moquette. These were built with them on the same production line usually at the end of the Alexander batch (and indeed overhauled at its Brown Street, Falkirk works, this continuing for Tiger Cubs even after takeover by SOL - this almost certainly being the reason for their retention in the SOL fleet), such as Alexander-bodied Tigers and for example the two 1955 Reliances B39/40 (SS 9615/6). Even some secondhand acquisitions came from Alexander.

In spring 1960, for whatever reason, Stark's suffered an acute vehicle shortage, and called at short notice on SMT to hire it a vehicle in order that it could maintain services, pending the delivery of its second new Tiger Cub, ESS 127. Stark's preference for anything Leyland was not

When independently owned, Stark's buses that made an appearance on the trunk Edinburgh-Dunbar service were painted in a version of SMT livery, and displayed SMT fleetnames and, amazingly, legal lettering! Seen in Dunbar is Stark's L9, a 1947 Tiger PS1 with 35-seat Alexander body identical to numerous SBG examples. Stark's retained its own style of two-tone green livery between 1952 and 1957 notwithstanding that SMT itself adopted light green during that period. The bus was withdrawn in 1961 prior to takeover. *Photobus*

STARK'S MOTOR SERVICES, DUNBAR
FLEET COMPOSITION AS ACQUIRED IN JANUARY 1964

Fleet No	Reg No	Chassis	Body	New
B39/40	SS 9615/6	AEC Reliance MU3RV	Alexander B45F	1955
C22	SS 7486	Bedford OB	Duple C29F	1950
F1	430 YTD	Ford Thames 570E	Duple (N) C41F	1962
F2	FSS 929	Ford Thames 570E	Duple (N) C41F	1962
F3	GSS 452	Ford Thames 570E	Duple (N) C41F	1963
F4	GSS 804	Ford Thames 570E	Duple (N) C41F	1963
H3	SS 7525	Leyland Tiger PS1	Alexander B35F	1950
H4	SS 8015	Leyland Royal Tiger PSU1/15	Burlingham C39C	1951
H5	EWG 240	Leyland Tiger Cub PSUC1/1	Alexander B45F	1953
H6	DSS 21	Leyland Tiger Cub PSUC1/2	Alexander DP41F	1959
H7	ESS 127	Leyland Tiger Cub PSUC1/2	Alexander DP41F	1960
H8	ESS 989	Leyland Tiger Cub PSUC1/2	Alexander DP41F	1961
T1	ESS 487	Trojan	Trojan C13F	1961

Notes:

C22: SS 7486 had a Ford 4D engine, subsequently replaced with a Perkins diesel unit

F1-4 were transferred to Highland in spring 1964 and were Highland's first Fords

H3: SS 7525 moved to the main fleet in May 1964

H5: EWG 240 had chassis number 520003 and was used as a Leyland demonstrator. Its remaining history is told in the captions. It was purchased by Stark's in 1956.

H7: ESS 127 was intended to be Alexander's PD 182 (OMS 258)

H8: ESS 989 is preserved and awaits restoration from a stock car transporter

H3/6-8 and B39/40 carried SMT livery whilst owned by Stark's for use on the Edinburgh-Dunbar service

The only new vehicle delivered to Stark's in Stark's livery after takeover was ZH529 in 1973. Because it was (incredibly) not fitted for one-man working, it was sparingly used and was eventually moved to Bathgate in 1978 where it deteriorated into a sorry state.

overlooked, and SMT incredibly sent ex-Lowland prototype Tiger Cub, H106 (LYS 943) to Stark's initially for a few weeks - Stark's already operated another prototype EWG 240, with Alexander B45F bodywork. Stark's second new Tiger Cub was scheduled to be tagged on to the end of the batch going through Alexander's coachworks for the Alexander company, as was commonplace, and indeed as happened to DSS 21, the 1959 new Tiger Cub. But because summer was approaching, it became clear that SMT could not extend the hire to await delivery of what turned out to be ESS 127, the 1960 Tiger Cub. A convenient arrangement was therefore struck with Alexanders, who had Tiger Cubs, to swap both ex-Lowland Motorways Tiger Cubs LYS 943 and FCS 451 for two AECs (which turned out to be Monocoach/Park Royal FMS 977/83) in May 1960. Effectively therefore the hire to Stark's was being 'carried' by Alexander. Now Alexander's own Tiger Cubs were just beginning to go through the coachworks and rather than wait to the end of the line, Alexander's PD182 (OMS 258) was hauled off the production line, registered in East Lothian as ESS 127 and painted into Stark's livery with Stark's intended Tiger Cub becoming PD182. The real twist, however, is that Stark's vehicle shortage coupled with the requirement to put the two Tiger Cubs through their first CoF in late 1960, appears to have been the catalyst for the Tiger Cub/AEC swap, somebody somewhere being clued up as to what was going on.

When Baxter's was acquired in 1962, its solitary Tiger Cub, also with Alexander body, SVD 113, was swapped for Alexander Reliance KWG 569 - it seems amazing that such vehicle swaps between SBG companies were initiated by a small independent suffering a vehicle shortage. As is so often the case, that is how things happened - generally unplanned, such interesting developments occurring 'on the hoof'.

The only Tiger, again a PS1, that came with Stark's was H3A, which survived long enough to be painted into Lothian Green and carry Eastern Scottish fleetnames. Its rounded windows identify it as a 1950 example, and is seen operating on a Bathgate service with a Midland Leyland PD3 overtaking it. SS 7525 was identical to a number of Alexander vehicles.
R H G Simpson

Stark's crack coach for many years was SS 8015, a 1951 Leyland Royal Tiger PSU1/15 with classic Burlingham Seagull C39C coachwork. Seen under SMT ownership as H4S with embossed Stark's fleetname, it sits on Edinburgh Castle Esplanade.
R H G Simpson

Leyland Tiger Cub prototype chassis no. 520003 started life in 1952 with a Saro B44F body registered ERN 776, and appeared at the 1952 Commercial Motor Show as the first of Ribble's large order. The body was moved to a production chassis, and 520003 was brought up to production standard and rebodied in 1953 with this unique Alexander B45F body, re-registered EWG 240 and demonstrated to various Scottish operators. It was bought by Stark's in 1956, and was withdrawn (as H5S) by Eastern Scottish in 1967 when it went to Lough Swilly Railway Co. It was not preserved. SS 8015 is behind in Dunbar. *John Burnett*

With SMT standardising on AECs, in 1955 Stark's purchased two Reliances with standard Alexander B45F bodies built alongside identical buses for the Alexander fleet. They were the first to carry the revised SMT livery which was exactly the opposite of SMT bus livery with light green roof and waistband for the Dunbar route, although they operated for the first two years with a dark shade of green in the same style. Seen as a Stark's bus, with SMT fleetname, SS 9615 (to become B39S) waits in Queen Street, Edinburgh. *R H G Simpson*

Shortly after takeover in 1964, four of the 1959 Reliance coaches, B670-3, went to Stark's, to replace four Thames Traders sent to Highland. These were originally repainted into light green coach livery but were quickly thereafter put into dual-purpose livery but in Stark's light green, and were fine vehicles. It is in Dunbar alongside C22, a 1950 Bedford OB which lasted until 1967 in Eastern Scottish ownership. B671 has been preserved in pre-Stark's coach livery. C22 is also preserved. *Gavin Booth*

Stark's took delivery of a new Tiger Cub in each of the years 1959, 1960 and 1961, all with Alexander bodies to Alexander fleet design right down to internal fitments and seating moquette. The first was DSS 21 which became H6S and it appears to have gathered up enough speed to overtake a cyclist on the A1 between Tranent and Macmerry on a three-lane stretch of road that is now a dual carriageway. It was built alongside Alexander's MWG-registered batch. *Photobus*

Each of the Tiger Cubs had differing central waistband arrangements. The 1960 example ESS 127, which was intended to become Alexander PD182, had the band continued round the front without a vee arrangement. It is seen crossing the Forth Road Bridge in August 1965 and before the Forth Bridges Motel was built on the open land in the centre left. *Gavin Booth*

The final Tiger Cub had a waistband arrangement that was otherwise only built for independent operators (including Carmichael of Glenboig) with a one-bay flash as on SOL vehicles (rather than Alexander's one-and-a-half) but with a vee moulding without the band continuing round the front. ESS 989 is on a short-working to Haddington and was built with Alexander's RMS-registered vehicles. It has been rescued from its fate as a stock car transporter, and let us hope it looks like this again one day.
Stewart J Brown collection

When a nationalised concern acquires an independent, the vehicle variety that comes into the fleet can be quite staggering. Many an operator would have discarded T1S, a 1961 Trojan with C13F body, but SOL took the view that if the bus got out of the depot under its own power it was 'a runner' and might as well be kept, and so it survived into 1967. It is seen at Dunbar depot. *Gavin Booth*

Stark's had four Thames Trader coaches, all with Duple bodies, which went to Highland Omnibuses after only a few weeks in the SOL fleet. These were popular coaches locally, and F3 has one of the final bodies built to this style and was new in May 1963. It is seen as Stark's T8 in Dunbar High Street. *Photobus*

The final Stark's Ford, delivered only two months after GSS 452, had this Duple Northern Firefly style body, the only one in the fleet. GSS 804 is clearly on a hire but is in an unidentified location, but it must be in late 1963 as the coach still retains Stark's flags on the front.
Gavin Booth collection

Although already illustrated under the Baxter section, C21S came to Stark's in May 1964 and went into Stark's livery. It was sparingly used, but is seen here at Levenhall, Musselburgh, working in on the Dunbar Express, introduced as a rail replacement service due to the Beeching cuts. Regulations at the time forbade driver-only working on express services! It is a 1959 Bedford SB1 with Burlingham 37-seat body, and was withdrawn in 1971, not going through its second CoF. *Photobus*

THE ALBIONS

POSTWAR ALBIONS have never been popular with SOL, and I debated with myself whether a separate section was warranted for them. Prewar, however, well over 100 Albions entered service in the late 1920s before the company went for heavier AECs and Leylands in the early 1930s. Indeed, with the Albions (logically) having an A prefix to their fleetnumber here lies the reason for AECs having a B prefix.

In 1955, SMT was desperate to find an economical vehicle for lightly loaded Borders services, the craze to save fuel still being uppermost in the minds of management. There was nothing on the market, so in typical SMT fashion it built one, and this turned out to be S1 (LWS 926), an integral SMT vehicle, with SMT B32F body which looked home-made, but most importantly with an Albion engine and transmission, and chassis number AL1, although one wonders if SMT25 was at one time considered! (The A fleetnumber prefix was now used by Bristols, so the S stood for SMT!) It ran for seven years (ie not going through overhaul) and was a contemporary of the Albion Nimbus. An identical body was built on a real Nimbus. The 1955 Motor Show had a production Nimbus on display in SMT livery, S2, but it was only on loan and no Nimbuses were purchased.

Then, still in its quest for a lightweight bus, in 1957 Albion produced the Aberdonian, which when bodied by Alexander with a standard body weighed well under 5 tons. This became S2 (the second) but it too was not deemed a success and it went to Alexanders, where it led a full life in the Aberdeen area.

But the search for a lightweight bus did not end there. In July 1959 a Bedford C5Z1 demonstrator XGD 509 with Duple Midland B30F body was inspected, and also in February 1965 SOL tried out EWT 385C, a West Yorkshire Bristol SUL4A, with the same Albion engine as the Nimbus, all to no avail. Finally the search for a truly lightweight vehicle was satisfied in 1967 when Bedford VAM5s entered the fleet.

It was only in 1965 that Albions entered the fleet in any quantity after the war. With SOL becoming disenchanted with the AEC Reliance 470, it was persuaded (possibly at gunpoint!) to accept 12 of the new rear-engined Vikings which turned out to be long-distance coaches. They too failed to make it beyond their first CoF, and were dispatched north after seven years to Highland and Northern, where again they survived somewhat better.

FLEET NO	REG NO	YEAR	CHASSIS	BODY
S1	LWS 926	1955 (1)	SMT/Albion	SMT B32F
S2	NSG 298	1955 (1)	Nimbus MR9	Alexander B31F
S2	RSC 427	1957 (1)	Aberdonian MR11L	Alexander DP41F
K1-12	DFS-C	1965 (12)	Viking VK43L	Alexander YC34F

In 1955, SOL was anxious to reduce fuel costs and it designed and built a small single-decker - what we would call a midi today - using Albion Claymore lorry running units. It was similar to the contemporary Albion Nimbus, and was bodied by SOL itself at Marine Gardens. A very similar body went on to a true Nimbus, and that has been preserved. S1 could hardly have been used on a less appropriate journey - a peak hour extra to Blackridge, on the trunk Edinburgh-Glasgow route - but that just typified the company. It lasted until 1962, not going through its seven-year CoF. *Photobus*

The only other Albions that were actually owned by SOL in the postwar years were 12 of the SBG-inspired Viking rear-engined design, effectively a rear-engined Tiger Cub. SOL's were C34F coaches, and were the first vehicles in the fleet with the script version of the Eastern Scottish fleetname, the 1964 Reliance coaches using Scottish Omnibuses. They too failed to make it beyond seven years, six going to Northern and the other six to Highland. YK2A (fleetnumbers had again reverted to 1) is in New Street depot when brand new. *Gavin Booth*

LEYLAND SINGLE-DECKERS

Leyland

PRIOR TO THE WAR, Leylands formed an important part of the fleet, with a large proportion of the heavyweight fleet consisting of Tigers in an almost 50/50 split with Regals. A large number of lightweight Cheetahs was also operated. After the war this all changed, and Leylands were very much in the doghouse. There are all sorts of stories as to why this should have been the case, but one which will not go away is that Leyland actually refused to sell SMT buses unless it could be guaranteed they would not be tampered with, particularly engine settings and other mechanical items which apparently resulted in some expensive warranty claims. The situation probably became impossibly inflamed when a number of Cheetahs were fitted with AEC 7.7-litre engines!

In any event, no new Leyland single-deckers entered service between 1940, when the last Tigers were delivered, and 1969 when six Leopards intended for Northern were diverted to SOL in a swap for Reliance 590s. In other words they were not ordered directly. The same year saw some Western SMT Leopards arrive secondhand.

Meantime, in past years, SOL had done everything possible not to operate Leyland single-deckers, and Tiger Cubs acquired from Lowland Motorways and Baxter's were quickly transferred to Alexanders, the full story of which is told in the Stark's chapter. It was only with the 1971 orders that Leopards were purchased new, and they were delayed by a year!

The searing desire of the SBG to dual-source led to the ultimate decision to run the Seddon Pennine VII, which can be read about under that heading. Most of the Leopards led very short lives - some as little as nine years before going for scrap despite time having proved them to be very sturdy reliable performers elsewhere. While the Scotmap exercise in improving efficiency undoubtedly was partly to blame, there was a real stigma attached to Leylands in the postwar years right up to the late 1970s when Nationals appeared. The 1974 deliveries and the 1975 London coaches only lasted a year, the former being replaced one-for-one by Bedfords, the latter by Seddons. The fascinating story of how Nationals came into the fleet can be read under the 1977 vehicle shortage chapter. It was only when the Seddon Pennine VII ceased production in 1982 and the introduction of the Tiger that Leylands appeared to be accepted without discrimination.

In a similar programme to the rebodying of AEC Regals after the war, in what I have described as Phase 1, a number of Tigers were also rebodied, the majority of these being allocated in the west.

After the war, no fewer than 52 1933 Leyland Tiger TS6s were rebodied, 25 of them by Burlingham with C35F bodies. Seen prior to delivery in 1949 is H70 in blue livery, these being among the final blue buses to enter the fleet. They were truly exceptional vehicles, and it is a pity that the majority went to the west where in time they were demoted to stage duties and poorly looked after. Let us remember them like this! *Gavin Booth collection*

ORIGINAL BATCH	VEHICLES REBODIED	BODY
H51-104 (FS 5573-626)	H51-8/60-76 (25)	Burlingham C35F
Leyland Tiger TS6 1933	H77-97/9-104 (27)	Alexander B35F
Burlingham B34R(H51-84)		
Metro-Cammell B34R(H85-104)		

A few other Tigers were rebodied, one with a Cowieson body (H175, ASF 387) and two rebuilt by ECW (H224/44).

The remaining 27 of the TS6s received Alexander bodies in bus form, and H88H is in Glasgow about to work to Airdrie in post-1957 style of livery. These vehicles were all taken off between 1959 and 1961, the Burlingham-bodied coaches lasting slightly longer than the Alexander buses. *Photobus*

FLEET/REGN NOS	YEAR	CHASSIS	BODY
H378-90 (VCS)	1963 (13)	Leopard PSU3/3RT	Alexander Y C38Ft
H391-3 (XCS 903-5)	1964 (3)	Leopard PSU3/3RT	Alexander Y C38Ft

The above Leopards came from Western SMT in 1969 and were converted to DP49F by ECW at Lowestoft

FLEET/REGN NOS	YEAR	CHASSIS	BODY
H394-9 (PWS-H)	1969 (6)	Leopard PSU3/3R	Alexander Y DP49F
H420-35 (YSC-K)	1972 (16)	Leopard PSU3/3R	Alexander Y C45F
H436-49 (YSC-K)	1972 (14)	Leopard PSU3/3R	Alexander Y DP49F
H476-90 (BFS-L)	1973 (15)	Leopard PSU3/3R	Alexander Y DP49F
H521-8 (BSG-L)	1973 (8)	Leopard PSU3/3R	Alexander Y C45F
H529 (BSG-L)	1973 (1)	Leopard PSU3/3R	Alexander Y DP49F
H530 (PWS-M)	1974 (1)	Leopard PSU3/3R	Alexander Y DP49F
H531-43 (BSG-L)	1973 (13)	Leopard PSU3/3R	Alexander Y DP49F
H544-53 (OSG-M)	1974 (10)	Leopard PSU3/3R	Alexander Y DP49F
H554-63 (PFS-M)	1974 (10)	Leopard PSU3/3R	Alexander Y B53F
H375-7 (HSG 564-6 N)	1975 (3)	Leopard PSU5A/4R	Alexander M C42Ft
N763-72 (BSF-S)	1977 (10)	National 11351A/1R	B52F
N862-71 (GSX-T)	1978 (10)	National 11351A/1R	B52F
N579-90 (RFS-V)	1979 (12)	National 2 NL116L11/1R	B52F
N301-10 (YFS-W)	1980 (10)	National 2 NL116L11/1R	B52F
H544-51 (BSG-W)	1981 (8)	Tiger TRCTL11/3R	Duple Dominant III C42Ft
H552-7 (MSC-X)	1982 (6)	Tiger TRCTL11/3R	Duple Goldliner C42Ft
H558-61 (PSF-Y)	1982 (4)	Tiger TRCTL11/3R	Duple Goldliner C42Ft
H311-6 (PSF-Y)	1982 (6)	Tiger TRCTL11/2R	Alexander T DP49F
H317-21 (TFS-Y)	1983 (5)	Tiger TRCTL11/2R	Plaxton C49F
L562/3 (A-BSX)	1984 (2)	Royal Tiger	Roe Doyen C42Ft
L564-9 (B-LSC)	1985 (6)	Tiger TRCTL11/3R	Duple Goldliner C46Ft
L322-9 (A-BSC)	1984 (8)	Tiger TRCTL11/2R	Alexander TE DP49F
L330-2 (A-BSC)	1984 (3)	Tiger TRCTL11/2R	Plaxton C49F
L335-42 (B-RLS)	1985 (8)	Tiger TRCTL11/2R	Plaxton C49F
L343 (C-WMS)	1985 (1)	Tiger	Duple Laser 2 C57F - Cummins L10

- All Leopards built from 1972 onwards had 680 engines: the others had 600 engines
- H530 was subject to an experimental negative earth anti-corrosion wiring system by Alexander delaying its delivery. It had the chassis intended for H489, which in turn had that allocated to H530.
- H544 (BSG-W) was a prototype Tiger. It went to Gibraltar for the launch demonstration by Leyland.
- L343 was a prototype Tiger and the first fitted with a Cummins L10 engine. It had a special chassis code
- H544-53 were sold to Midland in 1975
- H554-63 were sold to Central SMT in 1975
- H375-7 were sold to Fife in 1976

All of the ex-Western Leopards were converted to DP49F layout by ECW, but retained the slam door (what a mistake!), and could be seen at Lowestoft along with the 1969 VRTs that were constructed at the same time. ZH382A, rebuilt, is between Ormiston and Pathhead on the two-hourly service 121. It is during the 1977 vehicle shortage, and ought to have been driver-only. It was 30 minutes late, and the previous two journeys failed to operate - to which the author can testify, having turned up for them both! *Harry L Barker*

The first Lepoards ordered new by the company came in 1972, a year late. The first 16 were C45F coaches, but in later life they were simply repainted into dual-purpose livery without being reseated and were, apart from the seating, almost indistinguishable from the rest. ZH431A passes outside the Royal Scot Hotel in September 1980 inward from Ratho, along what is now a Greenway. *Harry L Barker*

The final 14 of the K-registered Lepoards came as DP49F, and ZH449A enters Gifford from Haddington bound for the 74-minute run into Edinburgh in early summer 1981, shortly before Scotmap alterations, and youthful withdrawal of this nine-year old bus. The blue Saltire-style fleetname and side advert despoil the vehicle. *Harry L Barker*

Airdrie bus station is the location of this shot, in typical Airdrie weather, of ZH483H, a 1973 Leopard, but from the 1972 order, all 15 of these having DP49F Y type bodywork. These were the final vehicles in the fleet to be delivered with non-reflective registration plates, albeit not of the white-lettered variety seen here! *Harry L Barker*

The true 1973 Lepoards had BSG-L registrations, and only the first eight were coaches. The final one, YH528A, is seen working as a driver-only bus near Ratho in the days when the bus grant dictated the use of coaches on stage mileage, hence the driver-only equipment being fitted. Note the dents in the roof! *John Burnett*

When BSG524L was repainted, it was not into bus livery. It appeared as an apparition in dual-purpose livery with bus seats and is seen near Lempockwells as ZH524A. When sold in 1982, it was one of the luckier ones and went on for further service as a contractors' bus with Hart, painted mid-blue, and for many years could often be seen stabled in Haddington. Such contractors must have regarded buses like this as a special gift. *Harry L Barker*

The other 1973 Leopards were all standard 49-seat dual-purpose vehicles, and were used on all sorts of duties from Airdrie and Bathgate locals to long-distance express routes. ZH543W is working the Edinburgh and Glasgow to Leicester service near Nottingham in August 1974, which it did for two years. Although the company was ahead of its time on the overnight London services, motive power such as this on an all-day long-distance service was found wanting. *T W Moore*

Two batches of Leopard came in 1974. Ten were B53F buses, and they only lasted for a year before being replaced by Bedford YRTs on a one-for-one basis. All subsequently went to Central SMT where their non-standard boots were a talking-point until some were panelled over. H561 is about to set off for North Berwick. *Harry Hay*

The final Leopards to enter the fleet, and the only 12m examples and also the only ones with Pneumocyclic transmission, were three 1975 M type London coaches. They too only lasted a year before going to Fife, being replaced by Seddons XS747-52. Here the final one, XH377A, displays its yellow and black livery well at Alexander's coachworks prior to delivery. Fleetnumbers were allocated after ZA374, the ex-Highland Bristol LH, rather than matching their registrations which would have been logical. This was possibly because they were only ever intended for a short stay, and the company did not want a gap of three in the fleetnumbers! *Gavin Booth*

The first Leyland Nationals to appear did so in November 1977, having been hastily diverted from NBC orders in less than a week. They are believed to have been originally destined for Crosville and entered service from Baxter's Victoria garage in this livery, the cream band being added locally. The lack of destination masking is noticeable. All of this batch were eventually repainted into dual-purpose livery to brighten them up, although to the writer this was not necessary. *Gavin Booth collection*

The ten 1978 Nationals were identical but came in dual-purpose livery. All went initially to Baxter's Victoria depot, and a shot in Airdrie shows N868V with a Leopard in the background. These vehicles were eventually dispersed to the Borders and Bathgate, and others were sold. *Harry L Barker*

There were even more National 2s - 22 in all - again in two batches. N589 is in Baillieston in July 1980. Again, all went to the west, but including Baillieston and Airdrie. Both this batch and the YFS-W-registered vehicles were dispersed far and wide across the UK, a more or less instant dislike to this model being detected and dealt with decisively. *Harry L Barker*

The Leyland Tiger chassis was introduced in 1981, and perhaps surprisingly in view of SOL's past record with Leylands, the company was chosen to feature in Leyland publicity for the model, and XH544A, one of eight Duple Dominant III toilet coaches for London service, went to Gibraltar for the Tiger's launch. It is seen here in the UK in the eye-catching blue Scottish livery. The frontal windscreen and destination design became known as 'SBG style' when fitted to Dominants. These coaches replaced the 1968 F-registered Bristol REMH6Gs. *Gavin Booth Collection*

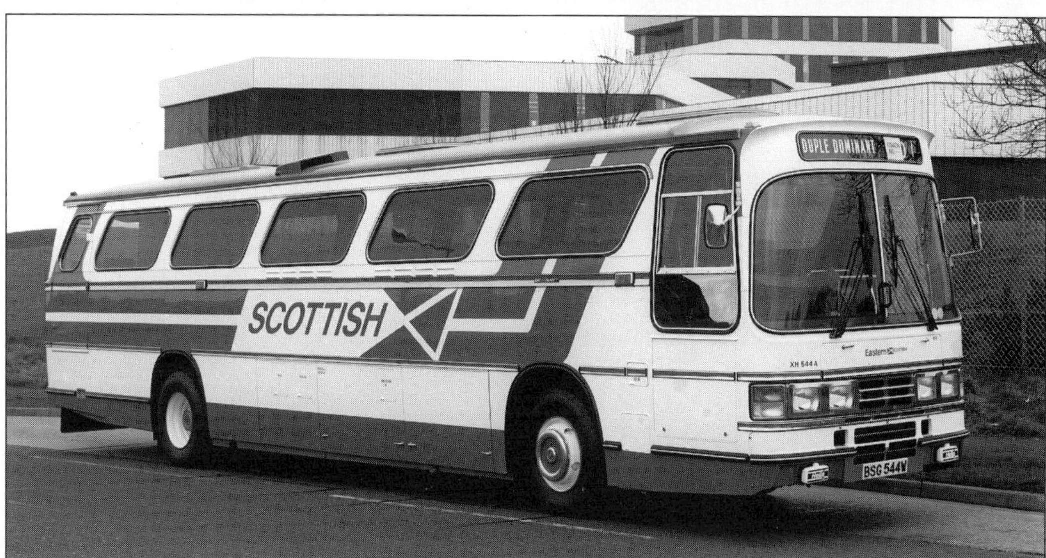

A further ten Tigers came in 1982, six with X registrations, and four with Y suffixes. These had Duple Goldliner bodies, being the highfloor design necessary for luggage space, which was not, of course, available to the same extent as on the rear-engined REMHs. XH557A shows the attractive lines of the Duple body, although unfortunately they were not as well contructed as perhaps they ought to have been. *Gavin Booth collection*

Also in 1982, six 11m Tigers came at a time when, following Scotmap, vehicle reductions and the huge influx of new vehicles in the 1978/80 period, meant that there was no requirement for new buses. These were originally ordered with Y type bus bodies and had they been delivered as such would have been unique. The body order was changed to T types to replace three-year old Seddons on the Edinburgh-Glasgow Express service, and here ZH315 is in a dedicated livery which four of these Tigers carried to good effect. These vehicles survived well into the Millennium with First Edinburgh running mainly out to East Lothian. *Harry L Barker*

Five Tigers came in 1983 and these continued the association with Plaxton built up during the Seddon influx from 1978. What would become YCH321A was the first SBG vehicle to carry a livery that was destined to be adopted as the standard for Scottish Citylink and is seen here in Ayrshire on an Omnibus Society tour in June 1983. These and three 1984 similar coaches had jack-knife doors. *Harry L Barker*

An experimental period in 1984 saw the arrival of two of the most impressive coaches to enter the fleet in the form of XL562/3, Roe Doyen-bodied Royal Tigers. Apart from adding interest to the London fleet, which always had been standardised, their classic design still stands the test of time today. Note the dark blue skirt - though it was probably not the intention to go back to two shades of blue appearance pre-1949 liveries! *Harry L Barker*

Eight Alexander TE-bodied Tigers also came in 1984, principally to replace high-mileage Seddons on long-distance Borders services. Looking very smart when new in May 1984 is ZL327K (L was used from 1984 to denote Leyland - H being abandoned) in Edinburgh bound for Melrose via the long route by Peebles. *Harry L Barker*

Plaxton returned to favour as supplier of coaches bodies in 1983, supplying Paramounts on Tiger chassis in 1983, 1984 and 1985. YL332 was photographed in Charlotte Square in 1985. *John Burnett*

DAIMLER DOUBLE-DECKERS

ALTHOUGH EDINBURGH CORPORATION TRANSPORT built up a large and successful fleet of postwar Daimlers, but eschewed and withdrew early AEC Regent IIIs, the opposite was the case with SMT. The only experience it had with Daimlers was after the purchase of Lowland Motorways in 1958, two CWA6s coming into the fleet (EE1/2) for a while. Baxter's of Airdrie had a Fleetline on order when taken over in 1962, and that bus was delivered directly to SOL complete with Alexander body in 1963, one of the first of the highly successful lowheight design. But SOL stayed loyal to the trusty Lodekka, and it was not until the 1970 orders (delivered in 1971), following the disastrous experience with Bristol VRs, that Fleetlines were to become the standard double-decker.

All Fleetlines ordered new were bodied by ECW. These proved to be good vehicles, but late deliveries due to London cornering the order book, and spare parts famines, took the shine off their attraction, and again because of the SBG dual-sourcing policy (the VR having been rejected) and an apparent dislike of Atlanteans, SBG influenced the design of the Ailsa which saw service with all SBG fleets except Northern, and this time Eastern was very much part of the double-deck dual-sourcing policy.

A number of the earlier Fleetlines had the back ends rebuilt with additional strengthening - the outriggers upon which the body was fixed were not up to scratch on a Fleetline ever since the first one was built in 1960, this being a design fault which was never properly rectified. All Fleetlines are recorded here - although the later ones were Leylands. Also the secondhand buses acquired from Central SMT in 1975 are included for ease of reference.

DD80 was moved eventually to Peebles depot for working schools journeys where it replaced driver-only FLF, AA876. It soaks up the autumn sun on 6 September 1980 in Peebles yard looking in remarkably good condition for a vehicle that would not last much longer. *John Burnett*

The 1972 order for Fleetlines was a year late, and all 20 of them came in spring 1973. With the ability to use these as driver-only buses, some went to the Borders for school duties, but use on other services between such service sees DD500D reversing away from the stand in Galashiels bound for the Wester Langlee housing scheme in May 1984. *Harry L Barker*

When Baxter's was acquired in December 1962, it had one Fleetline on order with the new Alexander D style of lowheight body and it was delivered directly to SOL in October 1963, seating only 73. It is leaving Glasgow on the trunk service to Edinburgh (which no longer runs). Ironically it was Western SMT that took the plunge in 1965 and ordered Fleetlines en masse, SOL sticking to the Lodekka. This bus was burnt out in 1965, and was rebodied with a standard 75-seat body in May 1966. It did go to Baxter's in 1964 as its no.79, the number that ought to have been a Bridgemaster, the original 'no.79' going to Red Rover. *Gavin Booth*

When DD961 was burnt out, one of Western's Fleetlines then being delivered was diverted to Baxter's, registered locally and became Baxter's no.80. DD80V is seen at Coatbridge beside beautifully painted FLF AA891V. *John Burnett*

Although ECW had introduced BET-style windscreens to Bristol VRTs, SOL continued to specify flat glass for its 1975-delivered Fleetlines (1974 order), and 25 came that year. The first three went to Baxter's in full Baxter's livery. Typifying a St Andew Square scene is a line up of Fleetlines with DD715A leading. Notice the bus station inspector with the white-topped cap. *Harry L Barker*

When the 1976 order for Fleetlines arrived in 1978, they were regarded as manna from heaven. There may only have been ten of them, but rarely has a batch of buses been so welcome. Seen crossing the River Tyne at Ormiston is DD860A in an in-house promotional advertising livery for the London express services. By this time, the company had succumbed to BET-style windscreens. *Harry L Barker*

The final 25 Fleetlines to arrive came in 1979 again with ECW bodies with BET-style screens. The Edinburgh-Balerno service worked every 15 minutes, and it is now combined with the Edinburgh-Wallyford route and other First Edinburgh services into East Lothian as the 44 group of routes. DD69A tramps through wet snow. *John Burnett*

FLEET/REGN NOS	YEAR	CHASSIS	BODY
DD961 (9961 SF)	1963 (1)	CRG6LX	Alexander H73F Ordered by Baxter's of Airdrie
DD80 (DVA 680C)	1965 (1)	CRG6LX	Alexander H75F Ordered by Western SMT
DD400-19 (USF-J)	1971 (20)	CRG6LXB	ECW H75F
DD281-300 (TGM 201J)	1971 (20)	CRG6LXB	ECW H77F Ex-Central SMT 1975
DD491-510 (BSG-L)	1973 (20)	CRG6LXB	ECW H75F
DD692-716 (KSX-N)	1975 (25)	CRG6LXB	ECW H75F
DD852-61 (GSC-T)	1978 (10)	FE30AGR	ECW H75F
DD51-75 (OSG-V)	1979 (25)	FE30AGR	ECW H75F

- Of the ECW-bodied Fleetlines, all had flat glass windscreens except DD852-61, 51-75 which had BET-style windscreens.
- DD961 was rebodied by Alexander as H75F in late 1965 after a fire, re-entering service in 1966.

THE SEDDONS

To consider the Seddons, all of which were of the Pennine VII model, it is necessary to go right back to the falling out of favour of the AEC Reliance in 1966. With the oft-mentioned dual-sourcing policy, it had thereafter been necessary for all SBG companies to purchase Leyland Leopards for their heavyweight underfloor requirements, that being the only heavyweight underfloor amidships-engined single-decker on the market. With no desire to continue to purchase lightweight buses, SOL too succumbed to the Leopard in 1969. Now, with Seddon having built the RU rear-engined model in the early 1970s because of excess demand for the Bristol RE, surely it could also build an underfloor amidships-engined model? Work therefore started on the Pennine VII.

Volvo, which was involved by the back door in the Ailsa project, got to hear about this and quickly imported the B58. It is no coincidence that the demonstrator BUS 653K was fitted with an Alexander Y type body to standard SBG specification, and it is equally no accident that it first came to SOL on demonstration ten months prior to the prototype Pennine VII being built. Hindsight is a wonderful thing, and we now know that the B58 was updated and refined into the B10M which for 20 years was generally regarded as being as close to perfection as you could get for a layout of this type. But the B58 was not chosen for the stage work envisaged by the SBG and it is probably true to say that it failed the Presbyterian SBG test by being 'foreign', and not being fitted with a Gardner engine. One can only imagine that it passed the operational side of things with flying colours!

It is often said that the Pennine VII is simply a Leopard with a Gardner engine, and indeed had Leyland offered a Gardner engine in the Leopard, the Pennine VII might never have seen the light of day. However, it is slightly lighter than a Leopard, and the initial ones were considerably more basic - it was designed as a simple reliable bus and I much prefer to consider it as an updated Bristol MW (only taken off Bristol's lists six years previously); is this what an MWL would have been like if Bristol had produced one? No spring-actuated handbrakes here on early models, and at first no automatic gearboxes.

The Seddons proved to be worth their weight in gold; they may not have been quite as sophisticated as a Volvo, but they certainly performed well, and were a major factor in extracting SOL from the horrors of its 1977 vehicle shortage. All ran a full service life, many up to 18 years or more, and a number survived at Borders depots into the new millennium. The ability of the Gardner 6HLXB engine to take low sulphur diesel was an added benefit.

Their fuel economy is legendary (a trade press test achieved a record 13mpg) and after some updating of the handbrakes, sorting out some initial clutch problems, and the introduction of semi-automatic gearboxes on late 1978 models onwards, these buses were probably better than Leopards. They were certainly faster than Leopards (and indeed some Tigers) with a fully-rated 180bhp Gardner 6HLXB bolted under the floorboards. S986 (allocated to Hawick) was the last Seddon bus to be built, and it is fitting that the final Seddons produced proved to be such a splendid vehicle. S602, XS750, ZS928, S936 and YS792 have been preserved. In all no fewer than 301 Pennine VIIs came to Eastern Scottish in eight years.

The prototype Seddon Pennine VII, ZS661A, entered service in early 1974 having appeared at the 1973 Scottish Motor Show. Always fitted with a bus rear axle, it was quickly used on driver-only stage services and is depicted in November 1977 heading for Gifford. It was off the road for many months in late 1980/early 1981 during its first CoF, as it was fitted with numerous one-off parts that were not carried through to production; it was partially rebuilt at the time to standardise it. *Harry L Barker*

The first production Pennine VII was ZS662A, and all of the N-registered vehicles came with high-speed rear axles. This July 1978 shot shows the vehicle used on stage service, the company only just beginning to recover from the 1977 vehicle shortage. Sister vehicle ZS671F has been produced as a 1:76 scale diecast model by EFE.
Harry L Barker

The KSX-N-registered Seddons came in three batches of ten, and the company still preferred the Y type for its top coaching work. YS673A, with a C45F body was used on stage service in the winter to work up mileage to satisfy bus grant regulations, and here it gingerly picks its way through Pencaitland shortly after a blizzard.
Harry L Barker

The first T types in the fleet came in the third batch of ten that year, and ZS688 has arrived in Oban in August 1977 on the Saturday-only service from Edinburgh, which had only one journey in each direction. The T type livery never seemed quite right and did not take advantage of the central waistband divide. All T types came as semi-coaches, there being no coaches with this style of body, although some were ordered.
Harry L Barker

1976 saw the arrival of the only 12m-long Seddons built, and also the only ones with the perhaps then dated Alexander M type body to C42Ft layout. Delivered in the blue and white Scottish livery, the introduction of Citylink livery resulted in the scheme seen here, which did them no favours at all. By November 1989, XCS749A is demoted to running within Scotland, but nevertheless providing a high degree of comfort for its passengers. Sister XS750 is preserved.
Harry L Barker

1977 saw the delayed delivery of another ten, and the final Y type coaches - the only vehicles that came in 1977 and the only vehicles with R registrations in the fleet. The final one was YS762F, and these gave good varied service, being downgraded to semi-coach without reseating, and some even converted to B60F school buses for the Borders. Linlithgow depot had S762, and kept it immaculate to such an extent that it went for further meaningful service to Stevenson's of Uttoxeter when withdrawn.
Harry L Barker

The first of the Plaxton coaches to be delivered in 1978 was a batch of 12 C45F coaches in the livery that perhaps suited them best of all - a cribbed NBC style. YS791C is seen on a tour. Sister vehicle S792 is preserved at the Scottish Vintage Bus Museum. These and the following batch were ordered as T type coaches, but delivery delays resulted in the body order being transferred to Plaxton.
Harry L Barker

FLEET	REGN NOS	YEAR		BODY
S661	OFS -M	1973	(1)	Alexander Y DP49F
S662-71	KSX -N	1975	(10)	Alexander Y DP49F
S672-81	KSX -N	1975	(10)	Alexander Y C45F
S682-91	KSX -N	1976	(10)	Alexander T DP49F
S747-52	MSF -P	1976	(6)	Alexander M C42Ft
S753-62	VSX -R	1977	(10)	Alexander Y C45F
S783-94	CSG -S	1978	(12)	Plaxton C45F
S795-811	DFS -S	1978	(17)	Plaxton C49F
S812-31	CFS -S	1978	(20)	Alexander Y B53F
S832-51	ESC -S	1978	(20)	Alexander Y B53F
S872-901	GSX -T	1978	(30)	Alexander T DP49F
S902-31	JSF -T	1978/9	(30)	Alexander T DP49
S932-41	LSC -T	1979	(10)	Alexander Y B53F
S942-56	LSC -T	1979	(15)	Plaxton C49F
S957-60	NSX -T	1979	(4)	Plaxton C49F
S961-6	OSF -V	1979	(6)	Plaxton C49F
S591-4	RSX -V	1979	(4)	Alexander Y B53F
S595-630	SSX -V	1979	(36)	Alexander Y B53F
S967-71	USX -V	1980	(5)	Plaxton C49F
S631-60	YSG -W	1980	(30)	Alexander Y B53F
S972-6	DSC -W	1981	(5)	Plaxton C49F
S977-86	JFS -X	1982	(10)	Alexander Y B53F

- S896-901, and all from S932 onwards (total 131) had semi-automatic gearboxes, the remainder (total 170) having ZF synchromesh gearboxes.

In spring and summer 1978, two identical batches each of 20 buses were delivered with bodies intended for Western SMT, hence the panoramic windows on 53-seat buses. The final two were S850/1 seen in Edinburgh having both worked express services as they had high-speed rear axles. The wrap-round advert gained favour for a while around the late 1970s and early 1980s. *Harry L Barker*

A further 17 Plaxtons followed in 1978, but these were 49-seaters and came in an unusual livery. Delivered without Y prefixes, which were later applied, S805A is on a tour. A number of this batch was used on the two-day London service initially - one wonders if they had been delivered with the intended T type coach bodies if this would have been the case.
Harry Hay

Typifying the later Plaxton deliveries on Seddons is ZS947, again new and prior to allocation, which is seen leaving St Andrew Square bus station presumably going off to New Street depot in view of the lack of passengers. None of the Plaxton-bodied examples carried the 'Seddon Gardner' logo. *Gavin Booth collection*

Plaxton continued to deliver Seddon coaches throughout the late 1970s and early 1980s, but to a C49F layout, and indeed all were treated as semi-coaches both in livery and fleetnumber classification. Seen in Peebles in May 1984 is ZS963 with the updated style of Plaxton body, when antimacassars still played their part in the nurturing of coach passengers. *Harry L Barker*

No fewer than 60 T type Seddons with DP49F bodies came in late 1978 and early 1979 in two batches of 30 similar vehicles. Although ZS896 was at the Scottish Motor Show, and along with ZS897-901 had a semi-automatic gearbox, the remainder were the last of the ZF synchromesh buses. Coming in from Penicuik when new, and prior to allocation to Linlithgow depot, is ZS873, the second to be delivered.
Gavin Booth collection

There were four batches of standard Seddon B53F buses, with short windows, wide four-leaf doors and semi-automatic gearboxes, totalling 90 vehicles in all. The first 10 came in 1979 registered with LSC-T marks, but later that year a further 40 identical vehicles arrived. These greatly improved basic stage services as past recent deliveries had featured mainly coaches. S627A is in Ratho in July 1987 on the service from Edinburgh in the livery where cream window surrounds improved the appearance of vehicles. Sister S602 has been preserved. *John Burnett*

The following year another 30 identical buses came, and these were widespread. S632S is at Quality Street, North Berwick in September 1983 taking passengers on the ex-Stark's service to Dunbar. New vehicles delivered to Stark's no longer wore that livery, but the depot still had Stark's legend over the entrance at this time. *Harry L Barker*

The final batch of Seddon buses ever built came to Eastern Scottish, being another ten 53-seat buses delivered in 1982. The final one, S986L, went to Hawick depot where it remained all its life, and the second last one, S985D, was allocated to Galashiels where it is seen reversing away from the bus station stance on the local town service to Wester Langlee housing scheme. The excellent condition of the bus defies its two years in service when this shot was taken in May 1984. *Harry L Barker*

THE VOLVOS

WHILE THE SBG had always had a 'mainstream' chassis - in the case of the double-deck fleet it was the Bristol Lodekka, replaced by the Daimler Fleetline, it equally had a secondary line. In the 1950 and 1960s it was the Leyland Titan, superseded by the Albion Lowlander. But the failure of the Bristol VR in SBG eyes resulted in a search for a secondary double-decker, at the same time as the work on the Seddon Pennine VII was being progressed. All of the SBG's eggs were not going into Leyland's basket, and so the Volvo Ailsa was born in 1973. Being a highbridge model restricted its availability, or so it was thought until some detailed reconnaissance was done!

The continual delays suffered in Fleetline deliveries meant that the 50 Ailsas ordered for Fife for 1977 delivery were split up, Fife only receiving six (1977) and Midland 14 also in 1977. The remaining 30 went to Western, Central and Eastern (ten each) when the delivery to Fife of 30 Duple-bodied Leopards was confirmed (see chapter on 1977 vehicle shortage). Their arrival in February and March 1978 was warmly welcomed by Eastern Scottish. That started the first of a very successful operation of the type, which later developed into purchasing a few Citybuses. Upon deregulation, secondhand Ailsas arrived from Western and Central, nine each from the same build as VV773-82 and South Yorkshire PTE also provided 25 bringing the total number of Ailsas operated to 83, and all from depots and on routes which were thought to be lowbridge only. These acquisitions are not detailed here as they fall into the post-1985 category.

VOLVO

Turning into St Andrew Square bus station from York Place is VV774W, one of the first ten Ailsas to arrive in 1978. These worked principally on the Edinburgh-Seton Sands service. Originally destined for Fife as part of an order for 50, 14 went to Midland, and only six to Fife. Fife then released the remaining 30, 10 each to Eastern, Western and Central, upon confirmation of its order for Duple Dominant-bodied Leopards. (See *1977 Vehicle Shortage*). *Harry L Barker*

The next Ailsas arrived in 1981, when 20 with the then new Alexander R type body were delivered, mainly to Dalkeith depot to replace the 1966 FLF6Gs, although some also went to Musselburgh. The busy routes to the south of Edinburgh left the bus station from Platform A, and VV87G loads up for another journey on the frequent service to Mayfield in July 1984. *Harry L Barker*

FLEET	REGN NOS	YEAR	CHASSIS	BODY
VV773-82	CSG -S	1978 (10)	Ailsa B55	Alexander H79F
VV76-95	HSF -X	1981 (20)	Ailsa B55	Alexander R H79F
VV149-58	B- GSC	1984 (10)	Ailsa B55	Alexander R H81F
VV169-73	B- KSC	1985 (5)	Citybus B10MD	Alexander R H84F

Further Mark III Ailsas arrived in 1984, this time a batch of 10. These buses had small but powerful turbocharged engines and gave excellent service for nearly 20 years. *Harry L Barker*

Underneath the similar Alexander R type bodywork the five Volvo Citybuses had a revolutionery chassis design with mid-mounted horizontal underfloor engines. These buses were 84-seaters. *Gavin Booth*

HOW THE COMPANY OPERATED

Edinburgh, where approximately one-third of the fleet was allocated, is a major tourist centre, and while tourism fell dramatically during the war, in the early postwar years it very quickly came to the forefront of the company's activities. The fleet expanded by approximately 150 vehicles after the war and there is no doubt that at peak summer times at least 100 coaches were required for tours, excursions and extended tours, in addition to the London services. Indeed, on reflection, 100 is probably an underestimate.

The most efficient way of dealing with such a seasonal demand, as far as vehicles were concerned, was to attempt to arrange fleet replacement in such a way that new vehicles were delivered in the spring or early summer, retain those that were to be withdrawn until autumn, and you therefore had an artificially enlarged fleet over the summer months. In addition, numerous coaches were delicensed over the winter. That was in theory. In practice it is true that many vehicles were delivered on time, and these invariably were allocated to Edinburgh New Street depot which used the buses, regardless of their type and suitability to the routes, all summer long giving them a good sound thrashing and a running in which at times must have been well in excess of the manufacturers' guidelines (or for that matter prudence)! One cannot imagine, for example, that Bedford envisaged the 1967 VAM5 buses with their 98bhp engines being used on Edinburgh-Glasgow express services, or that they would be out seven days a week from New Street from 6am (Mondays to Saturdays) to midnight many covering over 300 miles a day for the first five months of their lives! These buses clocked up between 30,000 and 40,000 miles during their spell at New Street before being sent to Kelso and Berwick.

Thereafter, in the autumn, the vehicles would be reallocated to the provincial depots and it was rare (although not unheard-of) for these outlying depots to receive brand-new single-deck buses; normally they received summer castoffs, perhaps four or six months old. It was not unknown for new vehicles to be delayed, and this caused vehicle shortages, which culminated in the 1977 situation, which is covered in detail later. Other shortages were catered for by purchasing secondhand buses from within the Scottish Bus Group, or, regrettably at times, by not running the fully advertised stage service, often by withdrawing duplicates at peak periods. This was especially prevalent in early summer when most coaches were delicensed, vehicles being taken off evening peak stage work to operate early evening tours on hot days.

In Edinburgh, staffing the summer peak was a major task and many long-serving crew members became tour drivers almost exclusively in these months. Thank goodness for the local university! Edinburgh New Street depot took on a huge number of students as drivers during the summer. Route training was sporadic, and at times non-existent, very much working on the basis that the conductor would probably know where to go, but if the conductor was also a student the passengers regularly had to stand at the front of the bus and give directions. I remember once having to draw a map and give written instructions to a student on the lengthy rural Edinburgh-Gifford service when I alighted from the last bus at night, there being no passengers left, but with 12 long rural miles still to go. At least the driver was conscientious enough to complete them rather than simply throw in the towel and go home.

Absolute pride of place went to the overnight London services and the company's first 8ft-wide coach came in 1949. B364A, an AEC Regal III with ungainly Burlingham FC31F body is seen here with its original front waiting in anticipation of departure from St Andrew Square. Note the destination arrangement. The Regal behind is one of the ten 1948 FFS-registered coaches with Alexander C30F bodies from batch B310-44, in blue. All of these were subsequently rebodied.
Gavin Booth collection

Because of the severe fluctuation in demand at certain times, there was an ever-present vehicle shortage particularly during the peak summer season. When the Royal Highland Show moved permanently to the Ingliston showground just to the west of Edinburgh, a 'reverse' park-and-ride service ran every few minutes for four days in June from St Andrew Square and every year necessitated the hiring-in of Lothian buses. This LRT 1974 Atlantean would be one of numerous similar vehicles on hire, and which were not just restricted to this route! *John Burnett*

Platform E on a busy day with six vehicles all pressed into touring duties. Good weather brought out the crowds and made anticipation of demand difficult which meant that the dual-purpose nature of most of the single-deck vehicles was used to true advantage. Reliance B806 (one of those originally intended for Highland) is nearest the camera in bus livery, with four other Y type Reliances (but only one in coach livery) and a Bristol LS. *Gavin Booth*

At the other end of the operational scale, B329E, a 1948 AEC Regal III rebodied in 1953 with a Burlingham FC35F body which replaced its Alexander C30F London duty body, connects at Kirk Yetholm green with the Saturdays-only one-man operated United Wooler-Kirk Yetholm service operated by a fairly new Bristol MW5G. *Gavin Booth*

MCW DOUBLE AND SINGLE-DECKERS

AGAIN IT IS DEBATABLE whether the few MCWs should have their own separate section, or be incorporated into the one-off section. I have included them here simply because they were part of the vehicle policy to experiment in the early 1980s, with the SBG having had a hand in the design of the double-deck Metroliner, rather than being one-off acquisitions. The Leyland Royal Tiger Doyens, and the two Olympian coaches with Alexander bodies, LL144/5, also fell into the experimentation role. In other words their appearance in the fleet, albeit for a short period, was deliberate rather than by chance!

While the original Metroliner double-deck coach went to Alexander Northern, members of The Omnibus Society had the chance to travel on it during that Society's Presidential Weekend in Scotland when it was new, and it was, believe me, very very impressive. It was the best advert MCW could have wished for due to the large number of informed industry 'experts' present - it was a unanimous hit as far as passenger ambience was concerned. SOL's dedicated London toilet coach fleet was getting long in the tooth - the Bristol REMH6G with M type C42Ft bodies were now at least 12 years old, and newer Tigers still sat only 46. A large proportion of the fleet lay idle during the week, or in the winter as peak demand varied widely. Utilisation was generally poor. The Metroliner double-decker had the potential to substantially reduce the fleet, but not capacity, as with coach deregulation numbers were rising. The only doubt was the engineering side and reliability of the vehicle. The possibility of a spanking and impressive new coach breaking down half way to London in the middle of the night, especially when it was unlikely a fully-laden one could be rescued by only one vehicle, was too much to think about. They were used on London services, but also on The Humber Scot from Glasgow to Hull, and the Edinburgh-Glasgow expresses. The single-deckers were directly compared with the Tigers and Royal Tigers. All the Metroliners had Cummins L10 engines. A further three Metroliner double-deckers appeared in 1986, but had short lives.

FLEET	REG NOS	YEAR	BODY
MM146-8	A--- BSC	1984	MCW CH69D
M333/4	A--- BSC	1984	MCW C46Ft

The Metroliner double-deck coaches were troublesome, and although initially intended for Edinburgh-London journeys, they ended up on the Glasgow Express service where they dramatically increased passenger comfort, and where they worked alongside Olympian coaches LL144/5. XCMM148A stands waiting to load in July 1984. These were without doubt the most impressive coaches ever owned by the company, albeit only for a short period. *Harry L Barker*

1983 was a very interesting year as far as coaches were concerned. Deregulation had resulted in a renaissance of that part of the fleet, and various experiments were undertaken. Two Metroliner single-deck toilet coaches appeared, and the first, XCM333A, is seen in posed position on what turned out to be its usual haunt, the Edinburgh-Inverness service, London being regarded as a bit cavalier for these coaches. *R H G Simpson*

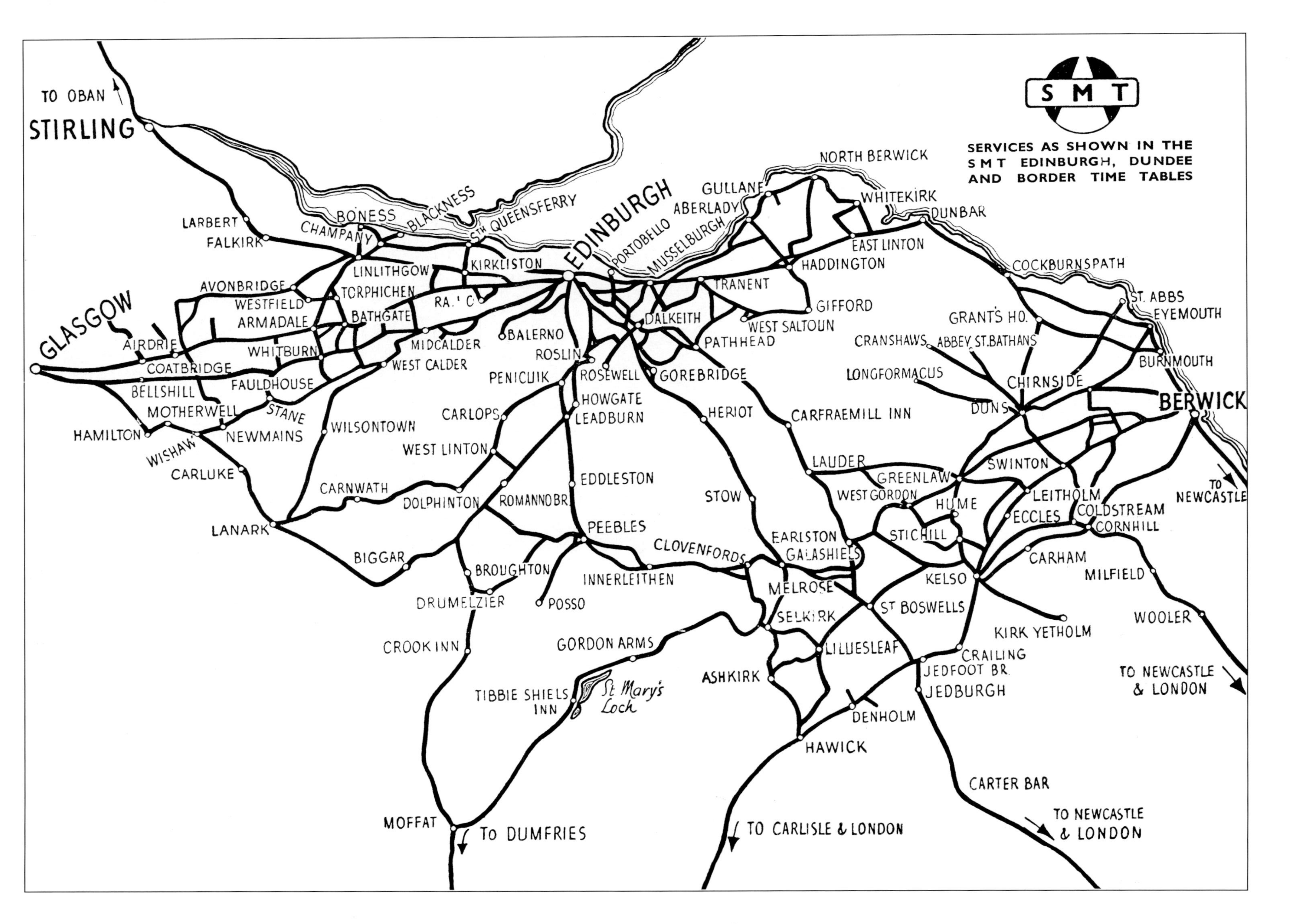
S M T
SERVICES AS SHOWN IN THE
S M T EDINBURGH, DUNDEE
AND BORDER TIME TABLES
TO OBAN
STIRLING
GLASGOW
EDINBURGH
BERWICK
TO NEWCASTLE
TO NEWCASTLE & LONDON
TO NEWCASTLE & LONDON
TO CARLISLE & LONDON
To DUMFRIES
LARBERT
FALKIRK
CHAMPANY
BONESS
BLACKNESS
S^TH QUEENSFERRY
KIRKLISTON
LINLITHGOW
AVONBRIDGE
WESTFIELD
TORPHICHEN
BATHGATE
ARMADALE
WHITBURN
RA.' C
MIDCALDER
WEST CALDER
FAULDHOUSE
STANE
NEWMAINS
WILSONTOWN
AIRDRIE
COATBRIDGE
BELLSHILL
MOTHERWELL
WISHAW
HAMILTON
CARLUKE
LANARK
CARNWATH
DOLPHINTON
WEST LINTON
CARLOPS
PENICUIK
BALERNO
ROSLIN
ROSEWELL
HOWGATE
LEADBURN
ROMANNOBR
EDDLESTON
PEEBLES
BIGGAR
BROUGHTON
DRUMELZIER
POSSO
INNERLEITHEN
CLOVENFORDS
STOW
HERIOT
GOREBRIDGE
PATHHEAD
DALKEITH
PORTOBELLO
MUSSELBURGH
ABERLADY
GULLANE
TRANENT
WEST SALTOUN
GIFFORD
HADDINGTON
EAST LINTON
NORTH BERWICK
WHITEKIRK
DUNBAR
COCKBURNSPATH
ST. ABBS
EYEMOUTH
BURNMOUTH
GRANT'S HO.
ABBEY ST.BATHANS
CRANSHAWS
LONGFORMACUS
CHIRNSIDE
DUNS
CARFRAEMILL INN
LAUDER
GREENLAW
WEST GORDON
SWINTON
LEITHOLM
COLDSTREAM
CORNHILL
ECCLES
HUME
STICHILL
KELSO
CARHAM
MILFIELD
WOOLER
KIRK YETHOLM
CRAILING
JEDFOOT BR.
JEDBURGH
CARTER BAR
ST BOSWELLS
LILLIESLEAF
DENHOLM
HAWICK
EARLSTON
GALASHIELS
MELROSE
SELKIRK
ASHKIRK
GORDON ARMS
St. Mary's Loch
TIBBIE SHIELS INN
CROOK INN
MOFFAT

DEPOTS

DEPOT CODES (see table on right) appeared as a suffix to the fleetnumber and were usually applied very diligently. In addition, there were sub-depots at Jedburgh (to both Hawick and Kelso at differing times) but under First Edinburgh it had a code in its own right, Melrose (to Galashiels) with buses being left overnight at various places, in particular Lanark and Biggar (subs to Edinburgh), Duns (to Berwick), Kirk Yetholm (to Kelso), North Berwick and Dunbar.

The Borders depots always had a very high standard of maintenance, and it is fair to say that their vehicles were rarely driven to the limit. Kelso depot was (even under First Edinburgh) renowned for sweeping out every vehicle between journeys, such was the length of layovers in this most rural of locations. Linlithgow depot, west of Edinburgh, was probably the best in the Central Belt, closely followed by Musselburgh and Dalkeith, a new depot opening at the latter in 1966 in the old station area replacing what went before. Broxburn was not that bad, trying its best to make a good job from appalling premises and conditions. Edinburgh New Street, at one time the largest bus depot in the country with almost 400 vehicles allocated during the summer months, had varying standards with, as always, coaches receiving preferential treatment. Maintenance was always a problem at New Street, and it was not unknown for anything up to 100 buses to be unroadworthy at some times of the year, most notably when they were really required. It is almost certainly from this aspect alone, which was seen by management, that the SBG's cautious vehicle policy was born - if it worked without maintenance, it was regarded as a good bus; complicated buses went wrong! This difficulty at New Street was caused, rather than exacerbated, by the shortage of buses. Quite simply there was no time for buses to be off the road for preventative maintenance, and they ran until they broke down, and were added to the non-runners in the bottom depot.

Bathgate and Airdrie were also poor, the former suffering from outside parking. Usually at Bathgate buses were left overnight with their engines running creating a diesel smog in the vicinity and resulting in the paintwork becoming discoloured to a bluish sheen when up against exhausts belching forth all night, every night. Bathgate also suffered badly from lack of staff, both mechanical and crews due to the then expanding BMC factory in the town which paid higher wages. Airdrie was a classic example of poor standards about which little was done largely because the distant Edinburgh management did not see on a day-to-day basis what was going on. On the other hand, Baxter's Victoria garage in the same town, maintained a reasonable standard.

By far the worst, however, was Baillieston. As noted under the chapter on the purchase of Lowland Motorways, a new depot was required in Glasgow to handle the local traffic gained as a result of its acquisition in 1958. Baillieston opened in late 1960, and immediately benefited from the allocation of the 20 1957 (ie nearly new) PD2/20s, coupled with a large number of new single-deck Reliances in 1960/1. In 1962 a substantial number of the new Bristol FLFs went there and approximately 80% of its allocation was under five years old.

Despite this the maintenance standards were very poor indeed, especially regarding bodywork where Baillieston (or perhaps I should say the good citizens of East Glasgow) had the ability to effectively destroy a vehicle in a matter of weeks if not days. These body defects were left unattended to largely due to the distance to the Marine Works at Edinburgh, and there is little doubt that such appalling standards would never have been tolerated further east, or by Central SMT or Alexander Midland.

When the Eastern Scottish fleetname was introduced in late 1964, the anomaly of having three depots either in Glasgow, or on its doorstep in the west, became clear, and it is probable that higher standards would have been attained if Midland or Central SMT had taken charge. This position is historical, and goes back to 1929 when Midland Bus Services of Airdrie were acquired.

DEPOT CODES

A	Edinburgh New Street
B	Bathgate
C	Dundee (until 1949)
C	Baillieston (wef 1960)
D	Galashiels
E	Kelso
F	Linlithgow
G	Dalkeith
H	Airdrie
I	Broxburn
J	Berwick-upon-Tweed
K	Peebles
L	Hawick (wef 1957)
N	Livingston (replacing Broxburn)
S	Stark's Dunbar and North Berwick
V	Victoria (Baxter's Airdrie)
W	Musselburgh (opened 1937 as WA indicating sub to Edinburgh - became W in 1955)

Bathgate: Although some vehicles could be kept inside overnight, by and large the majority were parked up in the adjacent yard, and there was always likely to be something of interest. Apart from Bridgemaster BB962A in the foreground, one of the 1960 LDs still in light green shows its rear end off. B708 and B452 can also be identified, the Alexander (Midland) halfcab Daimler sitting next to them is on an enthusiast tour. B98B is beyond that.
Stewart J Brown

Berwick: SOL shared Berwick with United, the depot being split into two halves, SOL's part being on the left, and they both looked out directly on to the bus station. Seen parked where the enquiry office used to stand are Seddons ZS758, another former coach, and S936, which has been preserved. Taken in September 1983, First Edinburgh now uses a yard in a trading estate in which to keep their vehicles, and there is little evidence of the depot or bus station. *Harry L Barker*

North Berwick: Stark's depot was always used to house SMT buses overnight, these being worked on the half-hourly service to Edinburgh, which was not joint with Stark's. As late as August 1978, and with five years still to go, Stark's name still appears over the depot, with Bristol LH6P preparing to make its 25-mile journey into Scotland's capital. *Harry L Barker*

The combined depot and bus station at Livingston replaced Broxburn depot in 1979. A line of buses sits on the pits, with two Bristol Lodekkas, two Daimler Fleetlines and, on the left, a Seddon Pennine VII. As a result of town centre redevelopment, the depot lasted barely 20 years. *Gavin Booth*

Melrose: This sub-depot of Galashiels was required to maintain the 15-minute frequency service to 'Gala', but was closed in 1965. Shortly before closure, B833D lies quietly looking out on to typical Borders countryside. It is a 1961 Reliance, and the curvaceous lines of the classic Alexander body contrast with today's offerings in bus design.
Gavin Booth

Two shots of Kelso: The depot was effectively the bus station with some additional parking space, there being two drive-through platforms. C742E, a Bedford YRT, and C568E a YRQ converted from a coach, face west in May 1982 and await their next duties, which at Kelso could have been some time away! The view of the depot facing east shows VAM5 C244E pulling away to Berwick in September 1978 in a typical Borders scene.
Harry L Barker

Two shots of Broxburn: Closed and replaced by Livingston, Broxburn went seriously downhill when closure was imminent. Taken only days before the event, FS6G, AA18, and YRQ, YC570, stand out of use on a Sunday in April 1979. Also, with apologies to all Brighton Hove & District fans, AA971 lies in a dreadful condition beside the depot. Note the rusting from leaks in the Cave-Brown-Cave system. *Harry L Barker*

Dalkeith: A new depot opened in September 1966 to which were almost immediately allocated 25 new Bristol FLFs, and 10 new Reliance 590s. Part of the depot was Dalkeith bus station and here two 1965 FLFs, a 1964 FS and a 1959 Park Royal-bodied Reliance are all visible. Note the differing 'Shop at Binns' adverts. *Gavin Booth collection*

New Street, Edinburgh: A 1965 shot of New Street with a line-up of 'deckers. the first two having been on route 70 to Penicuik. AA734G (obviously on loan from Dalkeith) is a 1959 LD6G, followed by two Central SMT PD2/1s, also on loan to meet the summer vehicle shortages, with three Regent IIIs, the first two Burlingham-bodied, the final bus having an Alexander body. An Alexander-bodied Monocoach is the single-decker in the background. *Gavin Booth*

New Street, Edinburgh: New Olympian HH127 emerges to greet the day with a journey to Penicuik. Had it turned right it would have lost its roof on the railway bridge under the East Coast Main Line just out of sight. Because access to the lower depot was under the bridge, it was well known that instant dismissal was the penalty for taking a 'decker there! The main depot was accessed by way of a curving ramp just up from this picture, down which it was thought highbridge 'deckers could not safely travel. New Street was closed after the management buy-out and the once-proud depot with at times over 400 vehicles allocated to it is now a car park. The company offices were situated above the depot. *Gavin Booth*

MARINE GARDENS AND THE MARINE WORKS

EVERY COMPANY OF reasonable size had its own workshops and SMT was no exception. Indeed, as it turned out, what went on at these works eclipsed some other larger companies with regard to initiative, daring and quality. During World War 2, at Marine Gardens, just north west of Portobello heading towards the then busy ports of Leith and Granton, was a pleasure ballroom complete with wooden floor which was converted to build tank landing craft as part of the wartime initiative. These were launched straight into the Firth of Forth!

Following the war, SMT used the Marine Gardens premises to undertake all sorts of bodywork repairs, overhaul and even bodybuilding, with chassis recertifications being undertaken at New Street depot. In the early 1950s, the bodybuilding activities flourished and following the purchase of some ex-London utility Guy Arabs in 1952, 23 were lengthened to 30ft and rebodied as 39-seat single-deck buses, 18 of these going to the newly nationalised Highland Omnibuses, and five to SOL itself (in 1954). It also rebodied an AEC Regent III (BB71, LWS 218) which suffered near terminal damage in an accident, and as noted elsewhere bodied the SMT-inspired S1 (LWS 926), similar to an Albion Nimbus, and also one real Nimbus.

Marine Gardens was also responsible for preparing vehicles during both major rebodying phases in the late 1940s and early 1950s of AEC Regals and Leyland Tigers. In particular, in phase two (see AEC single-deck chapter) it lengthened the chassis to 30ft and it is believed it actually bodied the Regals B330-44 under the guise of 'Dickinson of Dunbar', which firm may never have existed! It stored the original bodies from the Regals and rebodied older chassis with them. Bodybuilding activities ceased in 1956 (perhaps somebody in SBG found out what was going on, probably the group accountant!) with the Albion Nimbus registered NSG 869 (never an SMT bus) which is thankfully preserved. The Marine Gardens ballroom itself was demolished around 1961 and in its place the new Marine Works was built to encompass all overhaul and other heavy activities including chassis work. There really was very little that could not be done here.

In Spring 1962, the Marine Works opened with a special open day at which a number of new buses was displayed. These included prototype Y type Reliance B910, and recently delivered B909 of traditional style. New Bristol FLF6G AA883 was also there, this being one of the very first built with the new radiator grille. A Bedford VAS coach was also present.

The Marine Works became famous for the number of one-off experiments and engineering tinkering around and experimentation that was undertaken. Buses entered the Marine Works in a fairly organised manner thus: new; at two-and-a-half years for repainting; at five years for repainting; at seven years for first Certificate of Fitness (CoF); at nine-and-a-half years for repainting; at 12 years for second CoF; and only thereafter if required for extended CoFs (ie after three years) or repainting if necessary. The standard of buses coming out of the works, particularly after the CoFs, was truly exceptional. Almost a total rebuild was undertaken, including complete re-upholstery (sometimes including reinstatement of red seats on buses originally delivered with blue!), and in general attention to detail was superb even during repaints.

The vehicle fleet is characterised by alterations that occurred when buses went through their CoF, and the captions in this book make regular reference to this. Those close to the operational side will be aware that buses usually arrived at the works immediately after the Monday peak period, and depending how long they were in for - it could be two or three weeks for a CoF overhaul - everything that could be dispatched was to be out by 16.00hrs on a Friday. These buses were taken up to St Andrew Square bus station and used on peak service, giving the bus station inspectors some additional much-needed capacity on busy Friday afternoons. They were then sent back to their home depots by the Monday morning, but on summer weekends especially they would be used from Edinburgh as well!

In the early 1950s a considerable amount of bodybuilding and heavy engineering tasks were undertaken. 23 ex-London utility Guy Arabs were lengthened to 30ft and rebodied as B39F single-deckers, the first 18 going to Highland, the final five to SOL as D1-5. An unidentified vehicle is in course of rebodying at Marine Gardens in the early 1950s with a utility Guy beside it. *Gavin Booth collection*

MARINE GARDENS AND MARINE WORKS

This section lists principal projects undertaken in addition to its normal repair and re-certification activities

1942-45

Building of numerous bus bodies on utility Bedford OWB chassis. These included 60 for SMT, but also 102 for the Alexander group, and some for Caledonian of Dumfries. Many of these vehicles led short lives, most having gone by the early 1950s.

1947-49

The Phase 1 (see AEC single-deck chapter) rebodying programme, where no fewer than 101 prewar AEC Regal Is, and 52 prewar Leyland Tigers were rebodied by Alexander, Burlingham and Croft. The chassis to be dealt with were identified, original bodies removed, chassis overhauled and prepared for rebodying.

1947-48

Bodying of a number of Bedford OBs with coach bodies to a design similar to Duple's famous Vista, but differing from them in detail, most obviously the passenger door which slid inside the body rather than outside. 32 were built for SMT's own fleet (the final 18 being cancelled), with one for Mackenzie, Garve and others for W Alexander.

1952-54

The lengthening of 15 AEC Regal I and 50 AEC Regal III chassis to 30ft from 27ft, and preparing these for rebodying with full-front 8ft-wide bodies, 50 by Burlingham to its Seagull design, and 15 (B330-44) bodied by Dickinson of Dunbar. The removal and storing of existing bodies, mostly postwar, and transferring these on to older chassis for various SBG companies, but principally SOL itself, W Alexander and the newly-formed Highland Omnibuses.

1953

Conversion of a number of Bedford OB and OWB chassis to forward control thereby enabling the fitting of full-fronted Burlingham Baby Seagull bodies to 20 OBs of its own, and four OWBs for Highland. The existing SMT coach bodies built in 1947/48 were removed and some found their way on to other Highland OWBs.

1952-54

Following acquisition of 23 ex-London utility Guy Arabs, removal of the double-deck bodies, lengthening of the chassis to 30ft and building new B39F bodies to a very traditional 7ft 6in wide design, 18 going to Highland, and five to SOL itself. These retained their Gardner 5LW engines, but in typical fashion, it is more than likely that considerable tinkering with the chassis occurred, possibly even to the extent of replacing the well-used gearboxes with AEC units! These were allocated chassis numbers SMT1-23, although these were not carried.

1954

Following on from a serious crash, SOL's BB71, an AEC Regent III lost its Duple body and was rebodied by SOL to L53R layout. The chassis also came in for some attention, carried chassis number SMT24 and was re-registered LWS 218.

1955

The building of S1 (LWS 926), using Albion Claymore running units, similar to the contemporary Albion Nimbus, both underframe and body being SMT built. It lasted seven years, and was withdrawn before its first CoF.

1955

Identical body to LWS 926 built and placed on a real Albion Nimbus chassis, registered NSG 869 - the last SMT body built. This bus is preserved.

Major reconstruction and rebodying programmes were undertaken in the early fifties, AEC Regal chassis were lengthened to the increased legal maximum of 30ft. B392 was new in 1949 but was fitted with a new Burlingham Seagull body in 1954. The Bedford OB in the picture, C182 was built in 1948 with an SMT body. It was converted to forward control in the New Street workshops before being sent to Blackpool for its new Baby Seagull body. *Gavin Booth collection*

BB71 was badly damaged in an accident in 1953. Its Duple body was scrapped and its chassis rebuilt sufficiently for it to warrant new chassis and registration numbers. A new, 8ft-wide body was constructed at Marine, still seating 53. *Gavin Booth*

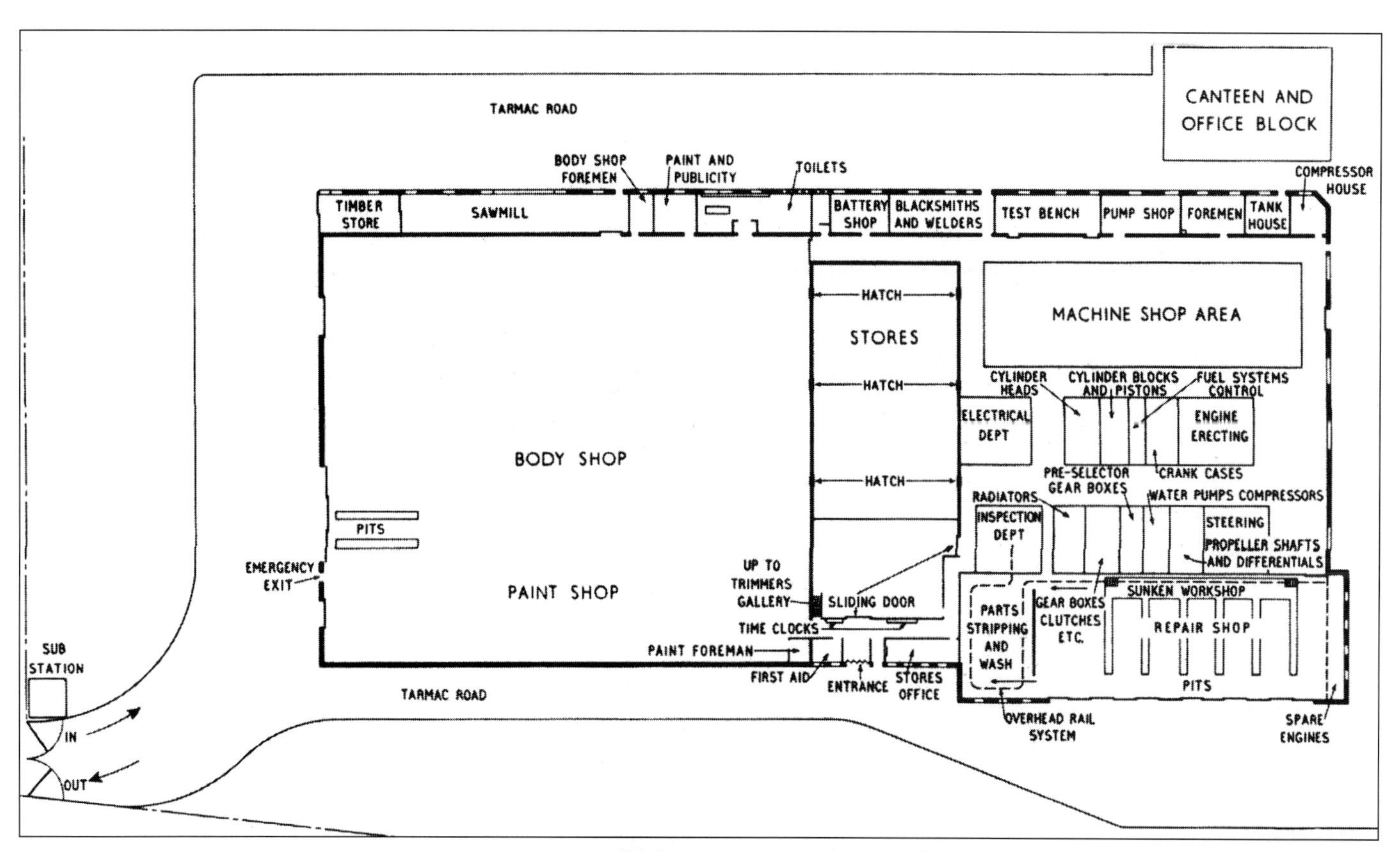

Marine Works floor plan from *Bus & Coach* magazine, June 1962.

Repainting was undertaken manually by brush and generally a superb job was done. Ex-Baxter's Bridgemaster BB18A, having just had its SBG style destination equipment fitted, is seen in a deserted Marine Works. *Gavin Booth*

At the same time, 1959 Park Royal-bodied Reliance B709 also glistens with a new coat of paint. This vehicle was allocated to a number of depots and appeared to have an itinerant existence. *Gavin Booth*

DEMONSTRATORS AND FIRSTS

DEMONSTRATORS CAN BE OPERATED or inspected either at the behest of the manufacturer, who would be wishing to impress a potential customer, or the operator being anxious to see something at first hand. Both are evident here, but the following is of interest.

The search for a lightweight rural bus for the Borders, the axing by SOL (and the year after by AEC) of the Reliance 470 in 1964 largely due to overheating difficulties, and the ever-present desire to have an SBG dual-sourcing policy led to some organised demonstrations. The story of the Volvo B58 is covered under the Seddon chapter, as it is undoubtedly part of the dual-sourcing policy, the Volvo being the loser. But perhaps more than any other UK bus company, SMT/SOL had a spectacular number of prototypes or one-offs or firsts, eg the first AEC Monocoach (building up the largest fleet in the UK); the first Bristol LS coaches with inward swinging doors to SOL specification, subsequently adopted as standard by ECW; S1, the unique SMT/Albion forerunner to the Nimbus; two prototype Tiger Cubs; the first production Bristol MW coach produced; the first 36-foot Reliance and the first Alexander Y type body (on the same coach); Bristol FLFs, believed to be the only ones built to take up the option of internal driver screen-changing; the first Bristol REMH vehicles built; the only Bristol VRTLL/ECW buses built; the prototype Seddon Pennine VII, and the first production one, and also the final Seddon bus built; a prototype Leyland Tiger and the prototype Tiger with Cummins L10 engine; the first Leyland Lion underfloor double-deckers (ordered before the 1985 split up). They were all here and amply demonstrate the pioneering nature of the company where very little was sacred on the engineering side.

Single-deck demonstrators were often used on the Edinburgh-North Berwick service, this practice continuing even after 1985 under different ownership when a Leyland Lynx appeared. None carried fleet numbers.

UMP 227, a Park Royal-bodied AEC Regal IV was used on the North Berwick service which often benefited from the use of demonstrators. The blue destination sticker gives the game away as to who it is operating for! No fewer than 75 Regal IVs were ordered, although 14 went to Western SMT to compete with Northern Roadways on its London service, resulting in only 61 entering service with SMT. *Gavin Booth collection*

The Edinburgh-Penicuik route saw an early AEC Reliance/Park Royal demonstrator in 1963 specifically to test out high-capacity single-deckers on an otherwise double-deck service. It had only been four years since the AEC/PRV combination had been shunned. *Gavin Booth*

A Bedford VAL14 with Duple Vega Major C52F body came in 1963 and was used on both the North Berwick and Glasgow Express services. No VALs were purchased, but VAMs did arrive in 1967. *Gavin Booth*

REGN NO.	CHASSIS	BODY	COMMENTS
LHY 949 *	Bristol Lodekka LDX	ECW H58R	To examine lowheight layout, 1950
UMP 227 *	AEC Regal IV	Park Royal B40F	To look at underfloor layout, 1950
13 DRB	Bristol Lodekka LDL6G	ECW H70R	Notts & Derby 30ft d/d test, 1958
XGD 509	Bedford C5Z1	Duple (M) B30F	Search for a rural bus, 7/59
995 EHW *	Bristol Lodekka FLF6B	ECW H70F	To examine F-series Lodekka, 12/59
80 WMH	AEC Bridgemaster B3RA	Park Royal H76R	To compare with Lodekka, 12/59
WJU 407 *	AEC Reliance 2MU3RA	Willowbrook C41F	Examined air brakes and coach body, 12/60
871 CBM	Bedford SB8	Duple C41F	Investment in coaches planned 1961, 12/60
327 NMP *	AEC Reliance 4MU3RA	Park Royal B53F	To try 36ft buses in service, 1963
7431 HN	Bristol REX6G	ECW B54F	As above, 1963
883 HMJ	Bedford VAL14	Duple C52F	As above, 1963
AWR 406B*	Bristol RELH6G	ECW C47F	Future London coach replacement, 2/65
EWT 385C	Bristol SUL4A	ECW B36F	Search for rural bus. 2/65
GFS 948D	Magirus-Deutz 150 L10		London coach trials, left-hand drive, 1966
FGW 498C	AEC Swift MP2R	Willowbrook B53F	Search for Reliance replacement, 10/66
OLH 302E	Mercedes Benz 0302	Merc. C43F	Trials on 2/3-day London service, 5/67
NHU 100F *	Bristol LHX6P	ECW B45F	Reliance replacement, 6/68
OEL 884G	Ford R226	Plaxton C47F	Reliance replacement, 12/68
PTW 170K	Ford R1114	Willowbrook B49F	Ford-inspired demonstration, 1972
BUS 653K	Volvo B58	Alexander Y DP49F	Search for heavyweight dual-source, 1/73
WXE 264M	Bedford YRQ	Alexander Y DP45F	Automatic gearbox, 12/73
MUT 206W	Dennis Dominator	East Lancs H76F	Fleetline replacement. 1981
OMS 910W *	Leyland B45	ECW H77F	Fleetline replacement, 1981
ABH 760X	Bedford YMQ	Wright B45F	Seddon replacement, 1982
A451 LCK *	Leyland Tiger 245	Van Hool Alizee C50F	To examine TL11 245hp engine, 1983
A308 RSU *	Volvo Citybus	East Lancs H83F	Ailsa successor, 1984

* Indicates that some positive orders resulted from demonstration.

West Yorkshire buses were often used by Bristol/ECW as demonstrators and in 1964 its AWR 406B was used principally on the Glasgow Express. Substantial RE orders followed, and no logical explanation can be found as to why more were not added instead of Leopards later on. *Gavin Booth*

AEC was aware of SOL's difficulties with Reliances, and in the absence of any AEC order in 1965, Swift demonstrator FGW498C with BET style Willowbrook body appeared, again on the North Berwick route. At least it had a destination screen fitted. *Gavin Booth*

Another West Yorkshire Bristol to appear was SUL4A EWT385C, with ECW B36F body, ostensibly for rural evaluation, but used on the North Berwick service. It arrives in Edinburgh with a Musselburgh allocated LD6G AA749W behind it. The SUL4A was withdrawn from Bristol's lists shortly afterwards, Albion ceasing making the engine. *Gavin Booth*

Not used in service, but attactive none the less, was Mercedes Benz 0302 coach OLH302E seen posed near Princes Street. Perhaps inevitably, none was purchased. *Gavin Booth*

This really was a demonstrator with chassis no. LHX001, and an experimental ECW body numbered EX12. The Bristol LH6P was requested to stand comparison with recently delivered Bedford VAMs and an order for 34 coaches followed. It would have been difficult to have found a less suitable service than that to Birkenside-running every 15 minutes usually with 76 seat Bristol FLFs. *Gavin Booth*

MCW's initial link up with Scania produced Metropolitan double-deckers and Metro Scania single-decks, but more unusual was the coach version as demonstrated by HOM 682L, which was used on the London service without success. *Gavin Booth*

Bedford YMQ / Wright demonstrator ABH 760 X in Waverley Bridge, Edinburgh passing prototype Seddon Pennine VII ZS661A. *Harry L Barker*

THE ODDS AND ENDS

One of the things which individualises companies is the number of one-offs and odds and ends in the fleet. Some companies tolerate them, others despise them. SMT had plenty of them, and while it is impossible to tell the stories behind them all, hopefully the captions sufficiently whet your appetite and create a flavour of how interesting and varied this company really was. The principal reason why so many one-offs and non-standard buses came into the fleet was entirely due to the vehicle shortage which plagued the company every spring and summer. Apart from those which were purchased, mostly from other SBG companies, those acquired from the takeover of smaller operators were apparently retained on the basis that if the bus could get out of the depot under its own power it was worth keeping!

A goodly number of buses which could probably justify being included here have already been incorporated into sections on the acquired operators, but there were secondhand London Guys, operated in original condition and then rebuilt as single-deckers by the company itself. Then there were the Tiger Cub swaps to Alexanders in exchange for a Reliance and Monocoaches. It was a regular occurrence for secondhand ex-SBG buses to be acquired for the summer season only to tide over anticipated shortages, these mainly going to Bathgate depot partly on the basis that there were a number of low-mileage duties there connected with mining contracts, and the BMC truck factory, and partly because it was perceived there was little point in destroying the company's own buses by sending them to Bathgate, it being more prudent to send someone else's there, such was Bathgate's reputation!

There were numerous hirings-in during the summer, and use of non-SBG companies' vehicles on stage service where layover was sufficiently lengthy - eg Ribble buses were regularly seen working from Edinburgh when visiting on the Scotland-Lancashire group of routes, although the use of United vehicles was never seen by the writer and it is thought that United itself forbade such activities. There are simply too many of these buses to detail individually, and to have done so would have required a greater knowledge and detail of record-keeping than I was able to undertake. The variety was astounding.

In 1951 SMT acquired eight utility Guy Arabs from London Transport, including E27, a 1945 example with Park Royal bodywork. The London red was quickly overpainted in light green, but they retained their white relief. In 1954 all eight were extensively rebuilt as single-deckers by SMT for its own and the Highland fleet. E27 is in St Andrew Square, when the centre of the square was used as Edinburgh's 'bus station'. *E Shirras*

Coastline was taken over in January 1937 and shortly after five Leyland Tiger TS7s with Brush B32R bodies were delivered to SMT having been ordered by Coastline. One original 1935 TS7, and two of the 1937 TS7s were included in the postwar rebodying programme and received 1948 Alexander bodies from the B310-44 batch. Always allocated to Musselburgh, their SY registrations distinguished them and here H209W departs on a peak journey to North Berwick, Musselburgh only working peak runs on this route. It was withdrawn in 1960. *Photobus*

Outwith the postwar rebodying exercise, other rebodied buses were rare. Following an accident in 1956, B456H, a 1953 AEC Regal IV, was rebodied by Alexander in 1957 with this style of coach body to London C30Ft layout, as it had originally been a London coach. Alexander used the current bus body shell for this and Reliance B547 which had a similar style of body. The SMT diamond on the front was rare. *R H G Simpson*

When Lowland Motorways was acquired in 1958, it owned two original Tiger Cubs. These went to Alexanders (see the Stark's section!) and were replaced by two 1955 Monocoaches with Park Royal B45F bodies from the Alexander fleet. Numbered B100/1, they added further interest in being renumbered to B37/8 in 1964 to make way for new Reliances intended for Highland! B38I is off on the infrequent service to Oakbank. *John Burnett*

In 1963 Highland Omnibuses, the recipient of a large number of utility Guys from both SMT and Alexanders in 1957 and 1958, needed replacements for these buses. 12 of SMT's original Lodekkas (AA3-14) were sent north, and replacement Bristol FS6Gs (AA943-60) were ordered. Due to delivery delays - ECW was well behind in 1963 - the FS6Gs were late, resulting initially in the Lodekkas running around Edinburgh in Highland livery! Highland L7 (ex-AA9) leaves Edinburgh for Dunbar, its five-speed box no doubt proving useful on the A1. After some weeks the Lodekkas went to Highland, and Highland Guys came south to Edinburgh where they worked for a few weeks pending delivery of the FS6Gs. *Photobus*

The return of utility Guy Arabs to the SMT fleet in 1963 from Highland Omnibuses was most unexpected, but the buses were put to good use. Highland E17, a 1943 Arab II with lowbridge Roe body that had started life with Alexander subsidary David Lawson before transfer north in 1956, is seen in Platform A of St Andrew Square bus station bound for Mayfield on the intensive group of services to the Dalkeith area. *Gavin Booth*

Alexander (Midland) MAC145 was transferred to SOL in exchange for ex-Baxter's Tiger Cub H3V. Its ordered existence shattered, matters were made worse by having an AH470 engine derated to 112hp from 126hp making it sluggish and unpopular compared to its fully-rated stablemates. Only the roof and waistband were repainted so it retained its cream window surrounds in similar fashion to RSC 427, the show Albion Aberdonian. B35A stands beside rebodied Reliance B698A. *R H G Simpson*

Above: 1959 Park Royal Reliance B698 had been wrecked in 1962 and was rebodied by Alexander with a Y type body in 1963 following on from B923-42, albeit to a slightly lower specification. It was officially converted to 2MU3RA standard by fitting air brakes. Some reports suggest it was burnt out, but the use of secondhand seats from the original discounts this theory. It went to fame by being involved in a number of subsequent crashes and even landed on the main Edinburgh-Forth Bridge railway line. Dalkeith depot initially refused to have the bus allocated to it under threat of strike action. It was taken off early in 1973. *AEC / Gavin Booth collection*

Above, right: There are not many AEC Regal Is that have sampled the delights of the outside lane of a dual carriageway, but in September 1964 when the Forth Road Bridge was opened, the adjacent cycle and pedestrian tracks were incomplete resulting in a special service being required over the bridge. B301A heads north having been reseated to B15F with room for cycles. *Gavin Booth*

From the 1950s an open-topper was kept on the books for special occasions, and originally this was Leyland Titan TD5 HH57, but in 1959 it was replaced by HH66. In 1942 the Ministry of Supply permitted the building from spares of 196 of the then current TD7 model, and one TD5, and this was the TD5 originally with Leyland-style Alexander L53R body. In 1971, after 39 years service, it too was superseded by AA5 (the second), an ex-Western 1955 LD6G registered GCS 245. DSG 169 is preserved in closed-top form in SMT blue livery as seen on page 5. *Gavin Booth*

The ever-present vehicle shortage resulted in regular purchases of secondhand buses from other SBG companies, many of which seemed to end up at Bathgate whose low mileage contract duties were well suited to them. Eight 1948 Central all-Leyland PD2/1s arrived in mid-1965, retained their Central livery and fleetnumbers and ran around until November that year. L379 leaves Edinburgh on the trunk service 16 with 'Glasgow' just visible on a paper sticker, the lower of the two on the bulkhead window. *Gavin Booth*

As CoFs ran out on these buses, replacements were found in the form of four ex-Western SMT PD1s, two with Leyland bodies, and two Northern Counties examples. One of the latter, HH48A was moved to Edinburgh, and is seen here resplendent in Lothian Green at Musselburgh Town Hall off to Gullane on a short-working on the North Berwick route. It survived for no less than four years with SOL until 1969. *Photobus*

Again in 1965 further SBG cast-offs were acquired, this time six AEC Regal Is from Alexander (Northern), all of which went to Bathgate. Here B41B, a 1947 bus with Alexander (Brown Street) B35F body and improvised radiator covering, awaits a departure to Greengairs, whilst the PD1/Northern Counties behind is HH49 from Western SMT. Both lasted into 1967. These vehicles were nicknamed the 'Tannochbrae Specials' after the *Doctor Findlay's Casebook* TV series. *Gavin Booth*

The sixth Regal to come from Northern was B46B, new to the independent, Sutherland of Peterhead. Also a 1947 machine, it has a Brush body, originally C30F, but reseated here to 35. Why it was necessary for such a large company to operate such elderly vehicles will probably never be fully understood. *R F Mack*

IN SMT LIVERY, BUT...

FROM TIME TO TIME, manufacturers are anxious to have their products seen by the industry in the livery of a fleet which they either considered as important or prestigious or where they really believed they could attract some orders. Because of the importance of the SMT Group to the industry, there are at least four such vehicles which fall into this category, and they cover types which never actually ran for the company or which were not purchased new. Flattery got you nowhere with SMT!

The first was HSD 473, an early AEC Reliance with Park Royal bodywork very similar to the 56 Monocoaches recently placed in service by SOL. Due to some problems with the Monocoaches, AEC was desperate to reassure the company that just as economic a vehicle could be produced with a separate chassis and body, and this bus was built for that reason. It went to Clyde Coast shortly thereafter, and was only withdrawn in 1972.

Two came from Albion, the first being a prototype Nimbus with Alexander body, Albion clearly hoping to win some orders following the SMT-bodied S1 (LWS 926). But it was not to be. Likewise, the withdrawal by AEC of the Monocoach in 1957 (SOL had standardised on the Monocoach for its single-deck bus duties since 1954, and had the largest fleet in the country at 95) led Albion to believe that it still wanted a lightweight vehicle, and with body orders having reverted to Park Royal for 1958 deliveries, Alexander was also anxious to show a vehicle in SMT colours. Accordingly at the 1957 Scottish Show RSC 427 appeared, an early Albion Aberdonian with one of the first of Alexander's attractive and comfortable straight waistline bodies that was set to become a Scottish standard. While it was actually owned for a very short period (unlike the Nimbus which was 'on hire') there is no record of either of these buses actually being used on service.

Considerably later, Dennis showed a Lance with an Alexander PS type body in SMT colours at the Commercial Motor Show in 1991. It was known that the then recently privatised company would be looking for major single-deck renewals with the ageing of the Seddon Pennine VIIs, but orders instead went to Volvo with its B10Bs, after which GRT Group vehicle policy was followed upon acquisition.

Although it was exhibited at the 1955 Scottish Motor Show in a version of SMT's livery, this Albion Nimbus/Alexander, numbered S2 and later registered NSG 298, was never owned by SMT.

At the 1957 Scottish Motor Show was another Albion in SMT colours, numbered S2. This was RSC 427, an Aberdonian with Alexander dual-purpose body. It susequently spent a full life with Alexander in the Aberdeen area. *Gavin Booth Collection*

Another Motor Show vehicle to appear in SMT livery was during the management buy-out phase when this 1992 Dennis Lance with smart Alexander PS B51F body appeared. It was never used, became J110 SPB and passed to Low Fell coaches in 1993. *Gavin Booth*

FLEET ALLOCATION AS AT MAY 1960

EDINBURGH (A) - Total 317

A1/2, 7-17, 29-32/8-44, 632-41 (34)

AA1-6, 608-21/42-51, 738-48/71-4 (45)

B 93, 104/9/10/33/5/6/8/42-5/63/92/3/6/8, 200/21/2/4/8/49-51/74-84/90-304/12-4/22/39/42/64/88/9, 405-24/9/30/9-55/7-79, 508/34-46/72/73/81, 658-66/70-9/98-708/75-85 (180)

BB79, 83-5/7-100 (18)

C156-75/88-202 (35)

H 69/70, 146, 208/9 (5)

BATHGATE (B) - Total 74

A21 (1)

AA582-5, 755-66 (16)

B113/55/8-91/9, 207/10-2/35/44/5/73, 325/8/54-60/2/3/94-6, 515/20, 714, 808 (33)

BB31-42/8/9, 65/6/8, 70-2/8, 80/2 (23)

S1 (1)

GALASHIELS (D) – Total 42

A5, 25 (2)

B141/9/50, 231-3/9-42/54-6/85-7/9, 319/26/36/7/65/9/70/2/4-6/8/9/83, 434/5/97-500/10, 716, 801 (40)

KELSO (E) – Total 27

A19 (1)

B147/53/94, 204/52/3, 310/1/23/30/8/85/6, 488/9, 506/75/6/8/9, 709/9, 800 (23)

D1-3 (3)

LINLITHGOW (F) – Total 40

A20 (1)

B152/6/7/61/8, 219/20/43/63-72, 305/6/21/45/6, 513/4/6-9/33, 667-9, 710-3, 805/6 (39)

DALKEITH (G) – Total 55

A18/27/8 (3)

AA7-15, 607, 734-7 (14)

B131/2/4/64-6, 201-3/8/9/29/36-8/60/1, 316/7/40/1, 504/5/29-31, 696/7, 804 (29)

BB 21-4/61/2/4/81/6 (9)

AIRDRIE (H) – Total 185

A33-7/45-50, 622-31 (21)

AA586-98, 600-5/52-7, 719-30/50-4 (42)

B44-50, 108/17/48/79/80/2-5/7, 226/30, 400-4/56/87/93-5, 501/2/22-7/47/68-71, 680-95, 786-95 (68)

BB 1-6/43-7/50-60/74-6 (25)

H 105-7 (3)

HH1-3/5-7, 548-67 (26)

BROXBURN (I) – Total 43

A23 (1)

AA599, 606, 767-70 (6)

B169/97, 246-8, 315/20/43/9-53/66/8/84/90-3, 511/2, 807 (23)

BB 25-30, 63/7/9/73/7 (11)

H 64/6 (2)

BERWICK (J) – Total 22

A22 (1)

B146, 258/9, 327/31-5/73, 426/7/91/2, 521/74/7/80, 796-8 (21)

PEEBLES (K) – Total 12

A3/24 (2)

B380-2, 428/31-3, 528, 718, 809 (10)

HAWICK (L) – Total 19

A4/26 (2)

B154/88, 234/57, 324/9/44/71/7, 425/96, 503/9, 717, 802 (15)

D 4/5 (2)

MUSSELBURGH (W) – Total 40

A6 (1)

AA731-3/49 (4)

B160, 205/6/62/88, 307-9/18/47/8/67/87/97-9, 436-8/80-6/90, 507/32, 715, 803 (31)

H 51/4/5/61 (4)

A	Bristol Single-deck	70
AA	Bristol Double-deck	127
B	AEC Single-deck	512
BB	AEC Double-deck	86
C	Bedford Single-deck	35
D	Rebuilt Guy Single-deck	5
H	Leyland Single-deck	14
HH	Leyland Double-deck	26
S	SMT/Albion Claymore	1
	TOTAL FLEET	**876**

1948 AEC Regal III/Burlingham B346 was still in the fleet in May 1960, allocated to Linlithgow. It is seen here in as-delivered condition, in the blue/cream livery of the time.

FLEET ALLOCATION AS AT JANUARY 1972

EDINBURGH (A) – Total 258

ZA31/3-9/41, XA169-74, ZA175-93, XA194, YA197-206, XA 272/4-9, YA319-43, XA349-67, ZA374, 623/8/30 (100)

AA29-32/7-40, 280-5, 747/8,50/61-6/9-74, 856-66, 943-55/7-60 (57)

ZB1-7/9-11, B26, ZB50/1/3-8, B80/3-5, ZB93-105/49/51/4, 683/4, B707/80, 800, ZB914/6, B918/20, ZB925/6/33/9/64 (53)

BB18, 962/3 (3)

ZC253/7-9/62/3, 450-8 (15)

DD400-9 (10)

ZH382-99 (18)

HH 42/5 (2)

BATHGATE (B) – Total 89

ZA49/50, 625-7/33 (6)

AA1-3/11-6/20/1/36, 308-11, 618-21/48-53, 734/5/55-60, 848-55/70-5/7-80, 956 (53)

B 5/78/9, ZB111, B541, 658-60, ZB685/6, B690/1/4/5/9, 717/84/97, 808/9/21/2 (22)

BB19/20 (2)

DD 412-7 (6)

BAILLIESTON (C) – Total 75

YA195/6, 347/8 (4)

AA41-4, 287-96, 579/80/6-90, 600-3/7-12/7, 885/6 (34)

ZB74-6, 107/19/20/50, 679-82, B718/88-95, 805/6/10-4 (27)

HH548-57 (10)

GALASHIELS (D) – Total 26

ZA638/9 (2)

ZB70/3, B829-33, ZB912/5, B917, ZB942 (11)

C233-7, ZC264-71 (13)

KELSO (E) – Total 18

ZA42/7 (2)

B88/9, ZB132, B702, ZB932/8 (6)

C238-44, ZC254-6 (10)

LINLITHGOW (F) – Total 37

ZA637 (1)

AA582/99, 606 (3)

ZB71/2, B82, ZB106/9, 110/47/8, B535/7-9, 662-9/92, 709/10/2/3/86/7, 819/20/8/95, ZB934/5 (33)

DALKEITH (G) – Total 75

ZA45/6, YA315/6, XA368-73, ZA631 (11)

AA28, 207-31/98-304, 889 (34)

ZB61/2, 108/12/55-9, B575/6/8, ZB674-6, B696-8, 799, 804/23-7/34, ZB936,7 (28)

ZC459/60 (2)

AIRDRIE (H) – Total 77

XA162-8, YA344-6 (10)

AA33-5, 286/97, 312-4, 591-8, 604/5/54-657, 719-25/7-30/51-4, 868/9/76/87/8/90 (43)

ZB63-5, 116/7/52/3, 678, B693, 775/6/8/83/98, 801/96-8, ZB927-30 (22)

DD418/9 (2)

BROXBURN (I) – Total 38

ZA43/4/8, 624/9 (5)

AA17-9, 305-3, 615/6, 736/7/67/8, 845-7/67/81-4 (20)

B544, ZB687, B703/5/6/8, 785/96, 807 (9)

DD410/1 (2)

ZH378/81 (2)

BERWICK (J) – Total 13

B87, ZB114/5, B921/40/1 (6)

C232/47-51, ZC252 (7)

PEEBLES (K) – Total 15

ZA635/6 (2)

AA45/6 (2)

ZB59/60, 688/9, B711, ZB910/1, B919, ZB922 (9)

C245/6 (2)

HAWICK (L) – Total 21

ZA632/40/1 (3)

ZB68, B81/6/90-2, ZB118/31/3/4, B781, 802/99-901, ZB913 (16)

ZC260/1 (2)

STARK'S (S) – Total 15

B39/40, ZB66/7, 670-3, B905-8 (12)

H6-8 (3)

BAXTER'S (V) – Total 45

AA8/9, 583-5, 613/4, 726, 891-4 (12)

B23-5, ZB27, B28-31, ZB32/3, B34, ZB160/1, B701/4, 902-4/9, ZB923/4 (21)

DD80, 961 (2)

HH31-3/7-41/3/4 (10)

MUSSELBURGH (W) – Total 40

YA317/8, ZA622 (3)

AA22-7, 642-7, 731-3/8-46/9 (25)

ZB77, B534, 714-6, 803/15-8 (10)

ZH379/80 (2)

UNALLOCATED

AA576-8/81 (4)

DELICENSED FOR DISPOSAL

AA4-7, B22,432/5, 501/3/11/22/3,5-8/40/2/6

HH34, YK1-12 (32)

A	Bristol Single-deck	149
AA	Bristol Double-deck	291
B	AEC Single-deck	300
BB	AEC Double-deck	5
C	Bedford Single-deck	5
DD	Daimler Double-deck	22
H	Leyland Single-deck	25
HH	Leyland Double-deck	23
K	Albion Single-deck	12
	TOTAL FLEET	**878**

ZH385, allocated to New Street depot, Edinburgh, in January 1972, was one of 16 Leyland Leopard PSU3/3R with Alexander Y type bodies transferred from Western SMT in 1969. *Harry L Barker*

FLEET ALLOCATION AS AT JANUARY 1982

(POST SCOTMAP)

EDINBURGH (A) – Total 163

XA354/7-9/61-3/6/71-3 (11)

AA970-3/85-7/91-3 (10)

DD 65-70/4, 287/91/3/5/7/8, 400/1/4/7-10/91/2/5/7, 500/3/6, 692-4, 700/1/6-9/11, 852/3/9-61 (42)

ZH420/1/4/5/8/30/1/5/47-9/83-90, H523/4/8, ZH536-42, XH544-51 (37)

S 620-8/39-46, ZS674/5/8/9, XS747-52, ZS758-61, YS785/6, 808/9, S812/45, ZS885-91/6-8, 915/25/6, YS942-5/65-8/72-6 (63)

BATHGATE (B) – Total 63

DD71-3, 289/9, 300, 413-7/96/9, 502/5, 713-6, 854-6 (22)

ZH429/32/9/40/4/6, H521/2/7, ZH529/30/2 (12)

S611-3/56-9, ZS672/83, 753, YS799, 805, S813-5/9/26/9/39/50, ZS876-9, 902-4, S932/3 (29)

BAILLIESTON (C) – Total 48

DD57-64, 292/4/6, 498, 857/8 (14)

N307-10, 585-90 (10)

S 654/5, ZS663/8-70/84/5, YS790/1, 811, S827/51, ZS874/5, 911-3, S936/7, YS954/5/64/70 (24)

GALASHIELS (D) – Total 27

ZC9/10, C569/70/4/5, ZC721/2/8/30 (10)

S603/31/60, ZS665/76/88, YS795, S823/43/8, ZS918-20, YS947/61-3 (17)

KELSO (E) – Total 16

ZC7, C568, ZC718/29/33/4, C742-5 (10)

ZS754, YS793, S821/44, ZS930/1 (6)

LINLITHGOW (F) – Total 30

C565-7/71/2/6, ZC717/23/4 (9)

DD411 (1)

S614/5/33, ZS662/71/80, 762, YS810, S822/5/42, ZS872/3/94/5, 916/7/21, YS948/9 (20)

DALKEITH (G) – Total 66

AA967/77-83/94/5 (10)

DD282/3, 403/12, 501/4/7, 699, 703-5 (11)

ZH426/7/41-3/76-9, H526, ZH531 (11)

S629/47/8, ZS673/82/90/1, 755, YS788/9, S820, ZS880/2/3/93, 900/22, YS951/8/9 (20)

VV76-89 (14)

AIRDRIE (H) – Total 80

DD75, 284, 418/93/4, 695-7 (8)

ZH399, 422/3/36-8/81/2, 533-5 (11)

N 301-6, 579-84, 763-72, 862-71 (32)

S595-602/51-3, ZS677/89, YS783/4, 803/4, S828/33, ZS905-8, S934/5/41, YS956/7/69 (29)

BERWICK (J) – Total 9

ZC727, C737/40/1 (4)

S608, YS796, S830/46, ZS927 (5)

PEEBLES (K) – Total 13

ZC6, 731/2, C738/9/46 (6)

DD286 (1)

ZS664, YS802, S849, ZS889, 924, YS946 (6)

HAWICK (L) – Total 17

ZC8, C564/73,ZC719 (4)

S 604-7, ZS666/7, 757, YS787, 806/7, S831, ZS928/9 (13)

LIVINGSTON (N) – Total 62

DD51-6, 281/5/8/90, 402/5/6/19, 508-10, 698, 702/10/2 (21)

ZH397, 433/4/45/80, H525, ZH543 (7)

S 591-4, 616-9/34-8, YS797/8, S816-8/34-8/40/1, ZS881/4, 909/10, S938-40, YS952/3 (34)

DUNBAR (S) – Total 18

C577/8, ZC725/6/35/36 (6)

S609/10/32, ZS756, YS794, 800/1, S824/47, ZS892, 914, YS950 (12)

MUSSELBURGH (W) – Total 32

ZC519/20, 720 (3)

S630/49/50, ZS661/81/6/7, YS792, S832, ZS901/23, YS960/71 (13)

VV90-5, 773-82 (16)

UNALLOCATED - WINTER STORE

ZC511-8

A	Bristol Single-deck	11
AA	Bristol Double-deck	20
C	Bedford Single-deck	60
DD	Daimler Double-deck	120
H	Leyland Single-deck	78
N	Leyland National	42
S	Seddon Pennine VII	291
VV	Volvo Ailsa	30
	TOTAL FLEET	**652**

N769, a Leyland National MkI, had originally been delivered to the former Baxter's Victoria depot at Airdrie (V), but was operating from the Clarkston depot at Airdrie (H) when photographed at Coatbridge. *John Burnett*

Tow Wagons

Like many bus companies, SMT favoured four-wheel drive AEC Matadors bought after military service, and one is seen in Princes Street, Edinburgh, with a Daimler Fleetline/ECW on tow. *Gavin Booth*

The former B361, a 1948 AEC Regal III/Burlingham became a breakdown lorry in 1960, and lasted in this form into the 1970s. It is seen in Princes Street. *Gavin Booth*

Baillieston depot's tow wagons had busy lives, and a former 1965 Bristol Lodekka FLF6G, tows a wounded Seddon out of Buchanan Bus Station, Glasgow. *John Burnett*

The four-wheel drive capabilities of the Matadors was useful on hills like Howe Street in Edinburgh, and this example, rebuilt as a halfcab vehicle, rescues a Seddon while another passes on the post-deregulation C23 service. *John Burnett*

THE 1977 VEHICLE SHORTAGE

IN CONSIDERING THIS heartbreaking phase of the company's operations, you really have to go back to 1975 and take into account the SBG decision-making process relative to the allocation of new vehicles amongst its constituent fleets, and couple this with the substantial vehicle orders being placed by the industry generally at this time.

This latter phenomenon was partly due to the generous Bus Grants scheme, and a fear that it might be phased out, and partly also to the postwar syndrome with all operators having out of necessity purchased a huge number of new vehicles after the war in the late 1940s. With the average life of a new bus being around the 15/16-year mark, replacements for these were effected in the early 1960s (this is when ECW got badly behind with orders), and they in turn were due for replacement in the late 1970s. Unless you wanted Leyland Nationals, there were delays in production across the industry of anything up to two years, and with the SBG using Fleetlines for many double-deckers and the inherent delays due to massive London orders, along with delays at Alexander affecting all bodies, partly also due to industrial action, trouble was brewing.

The SBG was allocated a number of vehicles by Alexander each year, and it was the SBG's decision who got what. Under this system Western SMT came out well on top - was there some internal politics here, SOL always in the past having been considered 'top company'? Western received very substantial deliveries of Pennine VII and Leopards, at the specific expense of other companies, notably SOL. This situation lasted for over two years. Meanwhile SOL actually lost nearly-new buses to assist in shortages elsewhere - a quick order for 20 Bedford YRTs saw these vehicles replace on a one-to-one basis one-year old Leopards to Midland and Central SMT. The 1975 Fleetlines were one-and-a-half years late.

A stranger in East Lothian in August 1977, a Western SMT Leyland Leopard PSU3/3RT with Alexander body, pressed into service with Eastern Scottish. It was one of four ex-North Western - later National Travel - buses acquired in 1977. *Harry L Barker*

Seddon however delivered its chassis timeously, as one would expect, SBG being its only major bus customer. With Alexander deliveries now behind by up to two years, the chassis were stored at both the Marine Works and at Alexanders coachworks. Because of space problems, there was no organised storage method, and the number of unbodied chassis rose to an incredible 129. These consisted of 40 B53F buses (two batches), 60 T type DP49F vehicles (two batches) and 29 coaches (two batches). In 1977 only ten coaches were delivered (the only vehicles in the fleet with R registrations, and coaches again receiving priority over buses), and these were a year late and are not included in the 129 chassis. Outstanding orders for Fleetlines totalled 35.

Meantime the company struggled on patching up Lodekkas that were over 20 years old for further short term (1-year or exceptionally 6-month) CoFs, these having to be used on all-day service. Vehicle reliability fell. The bulk of the shortage was felt at Edinburgh New Street depot, although all depots had terminally old vehicles. The press became involved and the company suffered some very bad publicity as a result.

After the 1977 session when the SBG decided SOL was only to get the 10 coaches mentioned above (surely somebody somewhere failed to bang the table hard enough), two lines of action were taken. The first was to try and get at least some of the Seddons bodied by another bodybuilder. That would not be easy - most bodybuilders would be reluctant to set up fresh drawings for a chassis they had never intended to body at a time of good order books.

ECW was the first port of call, 35 bodies on Fleetlines being outstanding with no firm delivery dates for the chassis. (The thought of an ECW-bodied Seddon, likened to an underfloor-engined Bristol, is mouthwatering!) ECW had been well-patronised by the company over the years and switching or delaying the Fleetline bodies on to other bodies for Seddons was the original not illogical thought, and the bus bodies on the 40 Seddons numbered S812-51 were the target. But ECW (apart from not having the capacity) was part of Leyland, and the Seddon was a product specifically introduced to counter Leyland dominance, and of course SOL had eschewed Leyland products deliberately in the past. Leyland is believed to have offered a very quick delivery of Nationals, which was rejected, but which became significant later on.

Then came Duple, which also was unable to meet reasonable delivery dates, but did suggest it could 'fit in' 30 bodies in early 1978, and these bodies were reserved on the basis that they would go on to something else if not required on Seddons. Duple certainly would not have wanted to build a one-off order on Pennine

VIIs, and it is believed that these bodies turned out to be the Dominant coaches going to Fife in 1978.

The search continued, and for the first time Plaxton came on the scene. Plaxton had never been the chosen builder of SBG coaches. It was not interested in putting bus bodies on Seddons - the Derwent was almost on the way out, and the Bustler was not yet available. But if it could break into the SBG coach market, it could well be worthwhile bodying some Seddons. Thirty vehicles were offered to Plaxton, but rather than body the dual-purpose Seddon order for 30 T types (S872-901) which was the original target, the 29 coaches were chosen at the last minute. These were to have had Alexander T type coach bodies (as distinct from dual-purpose) and one suspects that Alexander did not want to produce fresh drawings for these vehicles as to do so might cause further delay. (Plaxton did actually build 30, parts being already in situ, the 13th built going to OK Motor Services on an additional chassis, originally intended as a Seddon demonstrator). These vehicles (S783-811) were the pride of the fleet, and resulted in Plaxton building a number of coaches for many years to come for SOL.

The 40 buses (S812-51) received Alexander bodies diverted from Western SMT (identifiable by having panoramic windows) in early 1978. Because the chassis were stored tightly, they were bodied on a first-come-first-served basis, and these buses had coach-geared chassis with top speeds of around 65 mph (and used as such!), whereas 40 coaches or semi-coaches had bus-geared chassis, including many of S872-931, a goodly number of which spent their days pottering around on Bathgate and Airdrie locals, despite having semi-coach bodies, whereas the buses could be noted working Edinburgh-Newcastle service! Some of these vehicles were eventually regeared.

The second line of action was to acquire as many secondhand buses as possible, and the following 40 entered the fleet, including some incredible happenings which go down in history:

VEHICLES BOUGHT

6	Bristol Lodekka FSF6G/ECW H60F Ex Central SMT *AA430/7/8/41/4/8 (DGM 430, etc)*
12	Leyland Titan PD2A/30/Alexander H66R Ex Lothian *HH301-12 (YWS 601-3/6-8/10-3/7/38)*

VEHICLES HIRED (These did not carry fleetnumbers)

8	Leyland Titan PD3/6/Alexander H70F Ex Lothian *ASC 656/8/9/62/3/5/71/5B*
14	Leyland Leopard PSU3/3R/Alexander Y B53F Ex Central SMT *AGM 613-9/25B, KGM 647/8F, UGM 200/27K, XGM 447L, AGM 679L*

While the vehicle shortage was in full swing in the peak summer, the company was also blighted by recently introduced working practices whereby all weekend work was voluntary, and trying to match crews with buses, and attempting to get one-man equipped vehicles on one-man duties proved a nightmare to the extent that at times only an estimated 25% of services ran on summer weekends, and gaps of up to six hours on hourly routes could be found. Surely the worst job in the industry was an Edinburgh Bus Station Inspector! Passenger numbers fell sharply, never to recover. The Traffic Commissioners became involved, and management changes followed.

In Autumn 1977, just when the company thought the worst was over, and it had delivery dates for some new buses, Baxter's depot in Airdrie, which was about 50% one man at the time, voted to go completely one-man operated. This had to be implemented within a month, otherwise the agreement would have to be voted on again. But there were no suitable vehicles equipped for omo, conversions only ever being made as a last resort, even though by this time the company management actually was less hostile to, and indeed encouraged, omo. There was only one answer - take Leyland up on the offer of some quickly-delivered Nationals, and that is why Leyland Nationals came into the SBG. Had there been no vehicle shortage, it may never have happened.

A variety of liveries at St Andrew Square bus station in 1977 with, from left, Bristol FLF6G AA894 in Baxter's blue, Lothian Leyland PD2A/30 no.607 (soon to become HH305), and long FLF6G AA207 in standard green. *Gavin Booth*

Six rare Bristol FSF6G were bought from Central SMT in 1977, and AA438, still in Central colours, leaves St Andrew Square bus station for North Berwick . *Gavin Booth*

The same bus a few months later and now in Eastern Scottish green, picks up passengers in Balerno. This bus was withdrawn in 1978. *Gavin Booth*

The 12 ex-Lothian Leyland PD2s with Alexander bodies looked unusual in Eastern Scottish colours. HH301, formerly Lothian no.601, pulls out of St Andrew Square bus station bound for Polton Mill Road End. Note the revised style of grille fitted by Eastern. *Gavin Booth*

Eastern turned for the first time to Plaxton for bodywork to speed delivery of Seddons. YS791 is seen in 1981 against the backdrop of Glasgow's Buchanan Bus Station, which includes a selection of SBG types, mainly from the Central and Midland fleets.
John Burnett

The 1978 Plaxton-bodied Seddons were delivered in three different liveries. S810, seen in St Andrew Square, was in the dual-purpose version when photographed in August 1979. *John Burnett*

Newly delivered to the former Baxter's depot at Victoria, Airdrie late in 1977, are two of the first batch of 10 Leyland Nationals. These were SBG's first Nationals and were delivered in allover green. In spite of the vehicle shortage in 1977, only 20 new buses were delivered to Eastern that year.
Gavin Booth

POST 1985

IN ITS PREPARATION for deregulation, the SBG had a critical look at its operating companies, and perhaps not surprisingly in view of the geographical diversities of its operating territory, SOL was well and truly butchered. Baillieston depot operations went to Kelvin, a new company, and Baillieston was closed. Baxter's Victoria depot in Airdrie had already been merged with SOL's own Airdrie depot, and it went to Central, where I have argued it should have been from the start. Even that large depot closed totally in 1997. Linlithgow depot went to Midland working some of that company's trunk services out of Edinburgh with a modern allocation of Scanias and other Leylands. All of the Borders depots, plus the former Stark's depots at Dunbar and North Berwick, went to the new Lowland Scottish company, widely expected to be a Cinderella in view of its sparsely-populated operating territory.

How wrong could you be? The significantly lower operating costs now that the expensive Edinburgh operations were no longer carried in overheads proved that a viable rural company was possible. The rest - Edinburgh, Musselburgh, Dalkeith, Livingston and good old Bathgate - remained as Eastern Scottish Omnibuses, and was subject to a management buyout, a mere shadow of its former self.

Before the formation of Kelvin Scottish in 1985, Eastern's Baillieston depot was transferred into Midland Scottish control, and the former LL96, a Leyland Olympian/ECW, is caught at Buchanan Bus Station, Glasgow, in July 1985, still in Eastern green, but with Midland fleetnames and Kelvin fleetnumber O1. *John Burnett*

At first, many of the Eastern buses transferred to the new Lowland Scottish company in June 1985 continued to run in Eastern green but with Lowland fleetnames and numbers. Lowland no.10, formerly S610, is seen outside North Berwick depot in August 1985. *John Burnett*

Wearing Kelvin fleetnames on its Eastern livery, O8, formerly LL131, approaches Buchanan Bus Station in September 1985. *John Burnett*

Shortly after Eastern's Airdrie depot was transferred into Central SMT control, Central SP27, a Seddon Pennine/Alexander still in Eastern green, in Buchanan Bus Station in July 1985. *John Burnett*

Central SP13, formerly S905, a Seddon Pennine/Alexander T type, approaches Buchanan Bus Station in September 1985. Although still in Eastern green, it carries Central fleetnames. *John Burnett*

Photographed in Airdrie, the former Eastern Leyland National N866 as Central N53. This bus was sold to Western in 1989. *John Burnett*

LOWLAND SCOTTISH

LOWLAND SCOTTISH COMMENCED OPERATIONS in 1985, and it painted its buses in an attractive light green, almost an apple green, and primrose providing a highly relevant livery for an essentially rural operation. In fact, this livery was very close to that used initially on the prototype Y type, B910, when first delivered. However, the light green was short-lived, and Lowland adopted a dark green and bright yellow, not quite Lothian Green, but not far from it.

Some carefully planned reallocation of vehicles in the few weeks prior to the company's formation resulted in a well-balanced fleet! Under nationalisation, some limited vehicle purchases were made, notably two Alexander-bodied Olympian coaches, some TE-bodied Tigers, a Tiger coach and a Reeve Burgess-bodied Leyland Swift. Perhaps the most unusual were a trio of ex-Southern Vectis Bristol VRTs, the first to enter Scottish Bus Group service since the mass disposal of VRTs in 1973. The Border Courier services were renewed on contract, and some Reeve Burgess-bodied Bedford PJK (VAS to everybody else) entered service with the new company shortly after formation.

Lowland was then privatised, and a management buyout team was successful, and immediately started to renew the fleet with some Plaxton-bodied Scania K93s - a completely alien type of vehicle to the Borders! Some Optare MetroRiders appeared, and four Tigers with Alexander Belfast bodies and Volvo engines straight off the Ulsterbus production line, but as was the case with so many management buyouts, the company was purchased by one of the emerging groups, in this case the GRT group and standard GRT style livery, but using dark green and yellow, was applied. The merger between GRT and Badgerline has resulted in the company passing into FirstGroup, but the Scania theme continued by placing two Wright-bodied N113s into service - a far cry from the lightweight Bedfords of a few years earlier.

Lowland's main claim to fame during its management buyout phase was the acquisition of the independent Glass of Haddington. Glass's mid-blue, salmon and cream fleet was mainly single-deck based on Bedford coaches, but there were some heavyweights too, including some Tigers and DAFs plus Dennis Javelins. During the construction of Torness nuclear power station on the East Lothian coastline, the Glass fleet had expanded considerably, and had resulted in the purchase of Leyland Titan demonstrator VAO 488Y which passed into Lowland hands and was used on mainline service. Glass always had a hankering for stage routes, and operated a Saturday-only Haddington-Dunbar route via the hills for years, but during the Scotmap review in the early 1980s, took over peak journeys on the Pencaitland-Gifford-Haddington route from Eastern, and just prior to deregulation started up services from Haddington to Edinburgh in direct competition to Eastern. These were quite well patronised, the local goodwill element being substantial. The Glass name survived for some time on coaches under First Bus. Lowland was a tidy well-maintained fleet and a worthy successor to Eastern's Border area.

The original Lowland livery combined yellow with a light green, but this green was quickly abandoned in favour of a darker shade. Wearing the lighter green is no.943, a Leyland Olympian/Alexander RL type, seen in Haddington. *John Burnett*

Delivered to Lowland in 1996 following the formation of FirstBus were four Scania L113 with Wright lowfloor bodies. No.504 leaves St Andrew Square bus station on the lengthy Hawick service; these buses were quickly repainted red for the competitive Fife First service. *Gavin Booth*

Two Leyland Olympian with Alexander RL type bodies fitted with coach seating were delivered new to Lowland in 1987. No.902 is seen on an enthusiasts' tour in 1988. *John Burnett*

Lowland bought seven Dodge S56 with Alexander 25-seat bodies for use in Berwick-upon-Tweed. Branded as a Berwick Beaver, no.756 is seen when new in 1988 at Berwick bus station. It has dual-purpose seating. *John Burnett*

Acquired by Lowland from Ian Glass, Haddington, no.988 was a 1982 Leyland Titan TNTL11/1RF, built as a demonstrator. It is seen in London Road, Edinburgh in 1996. *Gavin Booth*

Freshly repainted in this 1996 view, Lowland no.158 was a Leyland National MkI acquired with the business of Lothian Transit. It is seen in Princes Street, Edinburgh. *Gavin Booth*

In 1991 Lowland bought four Volvo-engined Leyland Tiger with Alexander Q type bodies built to an Ulsterbus specification. No.303 is in St Andrew Square in 1997. Gavin Booth

DEREGULATION AND TOWARDS PRIVATISATION

THE REMNANTS OF THE nationalised company took delivery of its first Leyland Lions (and ordered three more) and also ordered four Citybuses with similar Alexander R type semi-coach bodies. Three Leyland Tigers also appeared. But most of its new vehicles were not to be full-sized. It was during this stage that two shades of green were introduced again - the central band on both single and double-deckers being light green.

Following upon the dismemberment of the company to embrace only the Musselburgh, Edinburgh, Dalkeith, Bathgate and Livingston depots, effectively surrounding Edinburgh, some real competition emerged in what turned out to be a vitriolic fight to the death with Lothian Region Transport (LRT), formerly Edinburgh Corporation. LRT decided to deregister a number of evening and Sunday services, and much to the delight of Eastern's management these were won on contract and it was possible to see Seddons and Ailsas working LRT routes. In addition, Eastern had prepared itself for deregulation by going down the minibus road, and in 1986 30 Renault S50 with Alexander bodies introduced a new five-minute frequency route running from Wester Hailes housing scheme in the west, right across the city to Restalrig in the east, and most importantly right along Princes Street. It seemed to be a success, with good loadings. A further 40 Renaults came in 1987, and the new city routes expanded into quite a good network.

At the same time, new conventionally worked services were introduced on an all-day basis resulting in new links within the city. Perhaps the biggest LRT mistake was to put out to tender evening and Sunday journeys on service 23 (Morningside-Trinity). This had long been LRT's most busy route - statistics readily available from past LRT annual reports show between 10 and 14 passengers per mile using the service and to this day, other than perhaps misjudgment, why it was deregistered will never be fully understood. Eastern won the contract, realised very quickly it was making serious money and soon started up an all-day operation matching LRT frequency. Eastern's C23 became its most profitable route, and a further 30 Renault S75s, but with Reeve Burgess Beaver bodies appeared, bringing the total number of minibuses to 100. I well remember standing at Haymarket, seeing Eastern Renaults pass heading westwards on a Saturday afternoon literally every minute or two, each one packed with standing passengers. LRT was being hurt. The conventionally worked services within Edinburgh were operated by Ailsas (with a few Seddons), and 18 Alexander-bodied examples from Western SMT and Central SMT, and 26 Van Hool-bodied examples from South Yorkshire arrived, many of the latter operating in cream and brown for some time.

So far, so good. But as has always been the case with the company, from its earliest days until acquisition by FirstBus, reliability fell far short of what was required and in some cases was downright appalling, especially on the conventionally worked city routes. Many of the Edinburgh bus station inspectors had grown up with the hands-on experience that if you are short of a bus, you hi-jack one which has just come into the bus station (it does not matter whose bus it is!) and worry about its next duty in a few minutes! Robbing Peter to pay Paul was the accepted practice, and Eastern simply did not have sufficient serviceable buses or crews available to work its advertised services. I recall vividly waiting in the rain for a C2 to Pilton in St Andrew Square from 17.10hrs until well after 18.00hrs and actually saw buses coming into the Square itself on the C2 being stopped by inspectors and redirected to the likes of Penicuik. After it happened three times, and a gap of an hour on a 15-minute frequency service, I gave up, and travelled LRT as did numerous other passengers who became distraught at the unreliability and the elderly buses now being operated. Meantime, LRT plodded on with its services, having extended many of these out of town to compete with Eastern - it has regrettably to be said with the blessing of regular passengers who knew they were now being offered a reliable service with reasonably modern vehicles (albeit with cold plastic seats). LRT did not alter the routes of its main trunk services which continued to cross the city as they always had done, and passengers liked the stability and predictable nature of their operation.

Eastern was one of a small number of operators to opt for the Leyland Lion. This was a double-deck version of the underfloor-engined Tiger built in collaboration with the Danish Leyland subsidiary DAB. These powerful and handsome vehicles proved to be a good buy and most of them were still in front line service almost 20 years after their purchase. LL176 was photographed when new in Edinburgh's Charlotte Square. *Gavin Booth*

Deregulation forced the whole bus industry to rethink most aspects of the way it operated. Minibuses were seen by many as the way to go and most operators purchased some. Eastern chose the van-based Dodge S56 with coachbuilt bodies by Alexander. These were used to compete with Lothian Region Transport on local services in Edinburgh. MR421 was new in 1986. *Gavin Booth*

Larger versions of the Dodge chassis, by now badged Renault, were purchased in 1991. These had 31-seat Reeve Burgess bodies and some were used to operate local services in West Lothian under the 'Bathgate Bairn' brand. *John Burnett*

Far from being the ideal tool for the job, Seddon S621 was photographed in January 1987 on local work in Comely Bank, Edinburgh. *John Burnett*

In 1988 the Alexander-bodied Ailsas were purchased from Central and Clydeside. These were built at the same time as the company's own examples. Many, like ex-Central VV45 were pressed into service in their previous owner's liveries. *John Burnett*

THE NEW SMT

EASTERN WAS PUT UP for sale along with all the other SBG companies, and it too was bought by its management who inherited an ageing fleet and an operation to which the tag 'could do a lot better' might well have been attached. LRT quickly saw the financial Achilles heel and expanded its out-of-town services further into West Lothian. Eastern, now a company laden with financial commitments, became barely profitable, and New Street depot had to go - it is now a car park. Although there was barely enough in the kitty to purchase new buses, the very satisfactory experience with the Volvo Citybuses led to an order for 13 Volvo B10Bs, one with a Wright body, the rest Alexander Strider. These proved to be a huge disappointment. Some Optare MetroRiders also joined the fleet.

I remember reading an article in the *Edinburgh Evening News* about the management buy-out of Eastern Scottish. It was immediately announced that the fleetname was being changed to SMT and I recall one member of that team being quoted on the basis that this was the easy bit. He was not wrong! The livery was changed back to dark green and cream, applied on an almost 50/50 basis.

The SMT fleetname with a modernised diamond was reintroduced. But the viability problems continued, and those watching the situation closely realised that the end was nigh. The GRT group, which by this time owned Midland (but not yet Lowland) purchased the company. In order to restore viability, a deal was struck with LRT to withdraw from West Lothian, on the basis that SMT would curtail its Edinburgh operations to some extent, but this included total withdrawal of the aforementioned C23.

Under GRT ownership, vehicle policy changed and 10 Optare-bodied Mercedes-Benz O.405 came into the fleet, followed by some other GRT types. Similar vehicles went to Lowland after the GRT acquisition, and inter-company transfers occurred between Midland, SMT and Lowland.

Twelve Alexander Strider bodied Volvo B10B, plus one with a Wright body, allowed a welcome modernisation of the fleet following a long spell with no new full-size service buses. They were used on the network of services between Edinburgh and West Lothian under the 'Diamond' brand; hence the route number's 'D' prefix. V202 was photographed in the now-demolished St Andrew Square bus station. *John Burnett*

The MetroRider was a much more satisfactory small bus than its van-derived predecessors and was purchased from 1992 to 1994. One of the earlier, narrow-bodied examples, MO511 was photographed on the short-lived tendered route from Ratho to Livingston in the spring of 1996. *John Burnett*

The unique Wright-bodied B10B, V213, operated out of Livingston depot when new but later moved to the Borders. Wrights would have been preferred for the whole batch but faster delivery gave the order for the first 12 to Alexander. *John Burnett*

Three Alexander B10Bs show the variety of liveries that could be seen before First's corporate colour schemes took hold. Nearest the camera 1210 still carries its original colour scheme; 1209 in the centre wears Grampian pale cream and SMT Lothians fleetnames while 1201 on the left is in First SMT deep cream.
John Burnett

The 1995 delivery of Optare Prisma Mercedes fitted in well with the fleet of similar vehicles operated by other Grampian group companies. M67 is seen near Riccarton on its way to Harthill in September 1995.
John Burnett

FIRST AMONG EQUALS?

Ten Pointer Darts were delivered in the end of 1997 with First corporate interiors before the Barbie livery was unveiled; they quickly adopted the new colour scheme. No.228 is seen at St Andrew Square in April 1998. *Gavin Booth*

Late model Atlanteans proved to be useful additions to the fleet in the late nineties most were Alexander-bodied examples from Grampian/First Aberdeen. An oddity was no. 759 on the left, which came from Hull via Glasgow. *John Burnett*

WITH THE MERGER of GRT Group and Badgerline, Edinburgh was totally surrounded by FirstBus companies - Midland in the west, SMT in the middle and Lowland to the east and south. But three management teams were controlling what one-and-a-half had previously done in SBG days, and the urgent need to address SMT's economic position, coupled with the essential need to produce some kind of an integrated network, resulted in the complete demise of the SMT company altogether, presumably on the basis that you keep the best and dispose of the worst. The management of SMT was divided up between Midland and Lowland, and the depots were allocated so that Musselburgh and Dalkeith went to Lowland, and Edinburgh, Livingston (now with a splendid new depot) and Bathgate went to Midland. The SMT name and livery was retained, but with Midland or Lowland legal lettering. Bathgate depot was closed.

During this phase, yet another new livery came on the scene - this time virtually all cream with an ill-placed medium green stripe round the buses. It looked paltry and insipid.

The company that we knew and loved had gone for ever, and the industry in Scotland will be the worse for it. With FirstBus also owning Glasgow and Central, everything that was SMT, including Baxter's, Stark's, Lowland and Coastline is now in FirstBus hands. At this stage we all wondered just how long the SMT name would linger on the buses - would indeed there be further rationalisation? Little did we know it, but we would find out soon enough.

Pressed into service even before all of its vinyls could be applied, no.73 was one of a batch of four Optare Mercedes delivered in 1997. They were intended for Midland but diverted to Lowland. *Gavin Booth*

FIRST EDINBURGH

IN WHAT WAS PERHAPS an inevitable, but also sensible, move FirstBus decided to establish a completely new company to embrace all the former Lowland, SMT and Midland operations and called it First Edinburgh. The relevance of the name to those in, say, Falkirk or Berwick upon Tweed, which is not even in Scotland, is debatable, but it provided the setting for a completely new start, which was probably required.

The livery situation was again looked at, and yet again it changed with almost the whole bus being cream, with green, yellow and blue bands at skirt level. While this incorporated the primary colours from each of its three constituents, it looked dreadful showing no imagination whatsoever. It was very quickly changed to include the FirstBus 'f' into the design, which only provided a minor improvement. There were soon so many liveries in the fleet that an untidy and unkempt appearance was projected.

The formation of First Edinburgh brought together Lowland, Midland and SMT. Yet another new livery was devised, using stripes of green, yellow and blue in a most unimaginative manner as shown by no.1051 in July 2001. *John Burnett*

The First corporate willow leaf feature of the Barbie livery made quite an improvement to the First Edinburgh livery. This has now been swept away by the universal imposition of First colours. *John Burnett*

When smartly presented the First livery conveys a fresh modern appearance. Examples of the types which qualified for this colour scheme included Wright-bodied Scania 584, Alexander Royale Volvo Olympian 1317 and repainted Pointer Dart 229. *Gavin Booth*

CONCLUSION

WHILE SMT MAY claim that there was not a level playing field with Lothian still being in local authority control, SMT effectively lost the battle and its current Edinburgh operations are a pale shadow of what was once one of the greatest operators in the country, from the UK's largest bus depot (also closed) in the city which still today boasts more bus use per head of population than any other in the UK. Perhaps history will show SMT, SOL and Eastern Scottish shot themselves in both feet repeatedly by giving absolute priority to tours and hires, and by not having enough vehicles to work their peak summer requirements thereby failing to look after their bread-and-butter passengers over the years. The company really believed, even as late as 1969 when I worked there, that there was an inelasticity of demand and if you failed to operate a journey, the passengers would still be waiting for the next one, and the company would still obtain their fares. Past practices spilled over into the deregulation era, where competition ensured they would not be tolerated, before the final LRT bullet through the head. The photos on the previous pages reflect the operations after 1985 in both nationalised and privatised form covering a spectrum of the remaining and new operations, with the captions telling their own stories.

With the changing and positive attitude towards public transport, hopefully we can look forward with some confidence to the future - but it will never be as interesting as the past.

THE AUTHOR

HARRY BARKER was born in July 1951 in Edinburgh, and lived for many years in the village of Pencaitland in East Lothian, approximately 15 miles from that beautiful city. However, he also went to school in Edinburgh (the Royal High School - which also educated Sir Walter Scott, Robin Cook and Gavin Booth!) and this necessitated daily travel by SMT/SOL bus on a 51-minute journey.

It was during these journeys to school that he became seriously interested in buses and SMT in particular, and he joined The Omnibus Society in 1967 where his interest flourished even further. He became secretary of the Scottish Branch of The Omnibus Society in the 1970s.

While a student, he worked with Scottish Omnibuses in its timetable department in New Street, Edinburgh, this being the company's head office as well as arguably the largest bus depot in the UK (258 buses in 1972). As the name suggests timetables, their compilation and the maintenance of up-to-date information was undertaken there (by John Weir), but this department was the real nerve centre of SMT. Next door but one was the assistant traffic manager, John Lamb, and one further door up was Archie Ross, the traffic manager. The timetable department also looked after all the tours activities under the tours superintendent, Ian Stephen, and all scheduling was under the control of George Sneddon. Not only that, but all insurance claims and accident reports were dealt with there (each listed under the individual bus, so a record of every vehicle's personal misfortunes was readily available!) and in addition the fleetlist was kept up to date by Frank Curran, this including additions and withdrawals and vehicle allocations, the majority of which were initiated from this centre of activity. There were regular discussions on staff shortages, one-man operation, maintenance problems, and the Bristol VRTs, which had just entered service. All in all it was a fascinating place in which to work - but Harry Barker took up banking instead.

Married with three teenage sons he moved to Yorkshire in 1991 from East Lothian (North Berwick) and he remained there until summer 2000 when he and his family moved to Tarporley in Cheshire. His financial experience stood him in good stead to become the national treasurer of The Omnibus Society which post he has held since 1988, and which he took up when a bank manager in the Scottish Borders.

Over the years he has kept very detailed records of the buses (and routes) of SMT and recognises that this is probably the correct time to release that wealth of knowledge to you, the interested reader. The detail that is evident is part of the fascination with SMT as there were many things going on which the casual observer would probably miss. Harry was able to travel throughout the company's network in the Edinburgh and Borders areas without a timetable, as he knew most times off by heart, and bearing in mind that many of the Borders services only ran on a few days each week, and different days at that, this was no mean feat. It is hoped that this work will prove to be a lasting and memorable tribute to one of the greatest and most interesting bus companies ever seen in the UK.